Studies in Educational Theory
of the John Dewey Society   **NUMBER 8**

The Educational Theory of George S. Counts

The Commission on Studies in Educational Theory
Appointed by the John Dewey Society

Frederick Ellis
Western Washington State College

Ward Madden
Brooklyn College,
The City University of New York

Israel Scheffler
Harvard University

Robert Mason, Chairman
Southern Illinois University
at Edwardsville

The Educational Theory of George S. Counts

by GERALD L. GUTEK

2Ω3560

OHIO STATE UNIVERSITY PRESS

To the Memory of Archibald W. Anderson

Table of Contents

Acknowledgments

I am grateful to the late Archibald W. Anderson, Professor of the history of education at the University of Illinois, who stimulated my interest and patiently guided the research and writing of this manuscript on the educational theory of George S. Counts. My thanks are also offered to Professors William O. Stanley, Harry S. Broudy, Joe R. Burnett, and J. Leonard Bates, of the University of Illinois, and Norman S. Graebner, of the University of Virginia, who read the manuscript and commented on it in the early stages of preparation.

I wish to express my appreciation to Professor George S. Counts who graciously shared some of his correspondence and manuscripts with me and who generously answered my many questions.

I appreciate the work of Professor Robert Mason and the members of the Commission on Studies in Educational Theory of the John Dewey Society in facilitating the publication of this manuscript.

GERALD L. GUTEK

Foreword

This work should be of tangible assistance in current efforts to redefine the role of the school in a rapidly changing American society. Not only does it reveal how an array of prominent educators sought to find guide-lines for education in two earlier periods of stress—the depression of the 1930s and the war years—but it clearly identifies George Sylvester Counts as one of the prime movers in this search. Since the names of many of Counts's colleagues of those days may be unknown to undergraduates in schools of education today, there is an additional gain in the descriptions of the views of Sumner, Beard, Bode, Kilpatrick, Childs, Charters, Hutchins, Washburne, Bagley and Kandel, particularly in instances where they agreed or disagreed with Counts. Organized approaches to education in those days—Progressivism, Essentialism, Reconstructionism, the Scientific Movement—bore designations that are still familiar, but this work provides interesting observations on their transformations over the past generation.

The central focus of the book, of course, is upon George Counts, whom the author attempts to explain but never to categorize. That is all to the good, because the first aim is possible of achievement (Counts has never been labeled a "mystic"!), but the second is impossible: Counts is unique. He has been likened to many profound and influential activists in our history, but he can be equated with none. His social philosophy has been cogently compared in other works with that of Thomas Jefferson, his concept of the school with that of John Dewey, and his manner of writing with Voltaire and Thomas Paine. The present volume uses occasionally what is perhaps the only proper term: "Countsian," but never in a worshipful sense. The writer does not hesitate to criticize Counts for his idealization of the "purity" of labor-class motives above the "selfishness" of the bourgeoisie, or for his over-optimism regarding the outcomes of Soviet social and educational reforms.

But it also points out some remarkable instances of farsightedness. As early as 1930, Counts saw the fallacy of the "separate but equal" concept in precisely the same terms which the Supreme Court recognized nearly a quarter of a century later. Through hundreds of speeches and articles beginning in the 1920s, Counts finally convinced most thoughtful Americans that our schools have *always* indoctrinated pupils. His early "radical" arguments that the school is more than an institution to train the mind, that it *should* undertake multifarious tasks in conjunction with other social agencies, but that it must not attempt to do everything—these views are held by millions of ordinary citizens today. Even his criticisms of teacher education in the late 1920s and 1930s have borne fruit in many states where requirements in "methods" have been modified and the traditional disciplines made less rigid. Nor should we forget that Counts was one of the few in those days who seriously urged the "educationists" to adopt some of the methods and procedures of the social scientists, a practice which is now almost *de rigueur*.

Perhaps the most valuable achievement of this work will turn out in the long run to have been the laying of the ghost of Counts's "softness on communism" and his "pro-Soviet ideology." The youth of today may never have heard these canards, but their elders should realize the absurdity and dangers of such accusations. For example, the writer of this Foreword was asked in 1944 by an agent of one of our investigative bodies if George Counts was "*still* a member of the Communist Party." The reply, although hopefully still recorded in the archives of the agency, is not printable, even now, in a work such as this. When the author declares that Counts, despite his frequent and sometimes vehement criticism of certain American institutions and practices, "never despaired of the efficacy of the American political processes," he is not only stating a demonstrated truth; he is offering a fine example for all of us to follow.

WILLIAM H. E. JOHNSON

University of Pittsburgh
July, 1970

The Educational Theory of George S. Counts

I. A Culturally Oriented Approach to Education

George Counts endeavored to formulate an enduring concept of American democracy. His analysis of American society during the depression was designed to serve a two-fold purpose: one, clarification of the American cultural heritage; two, formulation of a philosophy and program of education to meet the needs of a democracy in a technological age. Since he held that education existed as a function of a particular civilization during a particular historic moment, this analysis of American civilization was necessary for the subsequent development of Counts's educational theory. Exposition and analysis of Counts's theory of education during the 1930s requires a brief consideration of his "civilization-oriented" philosophy of education.

Counts based his theory of education on an interpretation of cultural relativism which was an outgrowth of the diffusion of pragmatic thought among American historians and social scientists. According to this interpretation, social and cultural development was particular or specific to the various climatic and geographical regions of the earth. Institutional life, too, developed as a particular response to varying environmental factors. As a social institution, education was conditioned by the values and needs of the particular civilization which it served. As historical-geographical forces had created great cultural diversities, so did these forces create great variety of educational philosophies and programs. American education reflected the conditioning factor of a particular environmental and historical development.

For Counts, the resources, potentialities, conflicts, institutions, and traditions of a particular civilization determined educational purposes, methods, and content. The civilization's history, perspective, and moral sentiments conditioned the particular educational philosophy. Further, Counts conceived of history as the record of change over time. According to this view, human history was the story of changing institutions, social relationships, and political arrangements. As one of these changing institutions, education was also changing, variable, and relative to a particular society at a given historical period.

Counts's acceptance of cultural relativism emphasized the particularities of a given society and the patterns of change unique to that society. Neither he nor the other relativists were concerned with patterns of cultural and institutional regularity. Rather they rejected the interpretation that society contained regularities of pattern and structure which are constant. Thus, Counts minimized the generalized institutional patterns and looked to the specific features which characterized a particular society. With this view of society, he rejected the concept of education as being constant, universal, or everywhere the same. Thus he rejected the philosophical orientations of Idealism, Realism, and Thomism and accepted a philosophic posture of Experimentalism within the framework of a pattern of cultural relativism. In *Dare the School Build a New Social Order?*, Counts warned that the conception of education as an essence eternally and universally constant contributed to the isolation of the school from political, social, and economic life.[1] Counts believed that education responded to changing purposes and conditions and assumed a particular pattern in every society and epoch. Thus, American education required an appropriate educational program. During the period of the 1930s, Counts urged the American educational profession to escape the coerciveness of economic aristocracy, accept democratic, egalitarian values, and organize life in harmony with the emergent reality of industrialized technological society.[2]

Under the influence of cultural relativism with its emphasis on the varying patterns of social and institutional life unique to particular societies, Counts conceived of a close relationship between group life and education. As a function of a particular society, education was to partake of group or associational life, as described in Counts's *The Principles of Education* published in 1924. Born into the group, man there acquired skills and knowledges which perpetuated the society and its members. Through the association of its members, group experience facilitated the sharing and transferring of experiences from one individual to the whole community. Shared knowledge, through common symbolic and linguistic patterns, became a cultural inheritance passed from one generation to the succeeding generation. Group association facilitated the discovery, accumulation, and utilization of an unlimited number of tools, skills, procedures, and appreciations. For Counts, like Dewey, education involved the transmission of these cultural instruments from generation to generation and thus served to perpetuate the life of the society.[3]

As he discussed the significance of associational life for

man, as a social and institutional being, Counts relied on the sociological theory of William Graham Sumner. As the group adjusted to environment, practices, customs, laws, and traditions accumulated. Folkways, past achievements conserving the successes of society, became authoritative sanctions conducive to social stability. Mores, derived from folkways, and regarded as good, true, and final provided instructional materials for the induction of the immature into the life of the society.[4] As the complexity of the cultural inheritance increased with material and symbolic accretions, specialized educational agencies and persons developed to instruct the child in the mores and folkways of the group. In *American Pragmatism and Education,* Childs said that for Counts the essence of education was the deliberate effort of adults to introduce the young to the folkways and thoughtways of their particular civilization.[5]

Although Counts appropriated the terminology of folkways, mores, and thoughtways from the sociological theory of William Graham Sumner, scant similarity existed between Social Darwinism of Sumner and the democratic collectivism of Counts. Sumner believed that the inherited patterns of folkways and mores were developed over long periods of time and were products of slow evolution. These products of cultural evolution could not be transformed through the deliberate or planned efforts of men. Counts, on the other hand, firmly advocated social planning and social engineering. His attack on laissez faire economics was in part a rejection of the theory of Social Darwinism which Sumner had advocated.

Nature of the School

Like Dewey, Counts viewed education as a process of inducting the immature into group life and providing experience
with the instruments of civilization. Accepting all forms of
human association as educative, education was not confined
solely to the school but proceeded wherever and whenever the
individual adjusted to environment. Therefore, other institutions performed educational tasks, but the school was specially
designed to do so.[6] For Dewey, the specialized environment
of the school simplified, purified, and balanced the environment. In accepting Dewey's description of the function of the
school, Counts added a fourth characteristic which already
seemed implied in Dewey. For Counts, the school also created
a graduated environment, consciously organized to facilitate
the gradual process of introducing the immature to society.[7]
Both Dewey and Counts agreed that the school simplified the
environment by modifying certain difficult and complex aspects of the adult world to meet the level of maturity of the
child. Its purified atmosphere banished certain harsh and cor-
rupt adult practices. The school further balanced and broadened the environment through which the learner derived perspective for evaluating and judging group affairs.

In describing further the nature of the school, Counts stated
that the school exercised both a residual and a normative function. In fulfilling its residual function, the school performed
those tasks and carried on that instruction which other institutions such as the family, state, or community delegated to it.
Institutions which once exercised an informal educative
function through the mediation of direct experience could no
longer fulfill this role in a complex and highly complicated

social order. As the immature member of society became more and more distant from the immediate experiences associated with institutional or occupational life, this learning was imparted through the indirect experience provided by the specialized institution of the school. Although other institutions such as the family, community, and mass media performed an informal educational function, the school existed as a specialized institution charged with the induction of the young as participants in social life through a graduated, balanced, simplified, and purified pattern of instruction or learning.

In describing the residual function of the school, Counts did not attempt to isolate the school from the other social institutions. His stress on institutional interdependence militated against a clear-cut and definite division of labor between them. Instead of a clearly defined institutional pattern, Counts rather emphasized the interrelatedness of social institutions and man's social and institutional life. As an agency functioning in an increasingly interdependent society, the school was to be clearly aware of its relationships to other institutions.

The residual function of the school which Counts discussed in "The Place of the School in the Social Order" can be further illustrated by a brief mention of Herbert G. Espy's *The Public Secondary School* and his discussion of vocational education and the practical arts. Espy discussed the demise of the relatively simple and stable social economy associated with rural and agricultural life. In the new industrialized social order of modern America with its growth of urban communities, its increase in national wealth, in the scope and complexity of industrialized life, and in exploitation of natural resources, the normal home environment of youth no longer provided opportunities for participation in the practical activities that adulthood demanded. According to Espy:

Specialization and large-scale production both in personal services and in the making of commodities, together with more convenient means of transportation, caused the complete disappearance of many of the characteristic activities of the home and the local community. These conditions also resulted in the development of different standards of workmanship in specialized occupations. In part, young people no longer found readily accessible the means by which they could develop the abilities and insights needed for competent participation in adult occupations, and the difficulties of gaining admission to vocational life had been increased.[8]

The accelerated pace of social change increased the residual function of the school as it performed tasks which had been administered in an earlier time by other social institutions. According to Counts, the taking on of these residual functions in no way hindered the specialized task of the school as an environment for the induction of the young into society. Indeed, awareness of the functions of other institutions and their transformation in the light of social and technological change was one of the aims that Counts urged the educational profession to assume consciously.

In speaking of the school's normative function, Counts meant that the school was inevitably concerned with the values of the society. Concerned with the good and bad, beautiful and ugly, prized or rejected, the school imposed the value schema of the society upon its charges. Returning to the theme of cultural relativism, this value schema or pattern was derived from the particular heritage of the respective culture and not from an order of reality which existed prior to or independently of the particular cultural milieu. Therefore, the first phase in the execution of the normative function was a study of the heritage and the contemporary culture to extract the value schema appropriate to that culture.

During a period of profound cultural transition such as that which American civilization was experiencing during the post–World War I era, the school faced a difficulty in execution of its normative function. Two patterns of civilization were in conflict as American society moved from an agrarian-individualistic to an technological-cooperative social order. With these two patterns of civilization appeared two conflicting set of values—one related to the old individualistic social order and the other related to the emergent collectivistic social order. Lacking a core of common agreement among those supporting the educational enterprises, the school faced a vexing problem regarding the appropriate value schema to impose upon the immature. Therefore, to fulfill its normative function the school was faced with two alternatives: one, the imposition of conflicting value patterns; two, choice between conflicting value patterns.

Counts called for educational statesmanship or vision and urged educators to choose between these conflicting value schemas. Through his particular interpretation of American civilization which was heavily influenced by the experimentalism of Dewey and the historical relativism of Beard, Counts postulated that clearly the emergent social order required the inculcation of collectivistic values. Therefore, the trend of social change necessitated that the school impose the values of the coming age.

Counts rejected the alternatives of objectivity or complete partiality between competing value patterns. Even if theoretically possible, such a duality in values would not fulfill the task of creating balanced and harmonious individuals. The school would not balance but would perpetuate the split which rent American society and was a basic ingredient in social, economic, and political disorder. To execute the first phase of the normative function, the imposition of a value schema, the school had to choose between competing sets of values. In *Dare the School Build a New Social Order?,* Counts definitely urged educators to make a commitment to the collectivistic values which he believed characterized the emergent social order.

Finally, in consideration of the residual and normative functions of the school, Counts rejected the idea of complete institutional autonomy. In a complex civilization, the school took on subsidiary functions which were once performed by other institutions. However, as the school sought to impose a particular value pattern, it also would transform the functions of the institutions of society. For example, the role of government in the cooperative society would be vastly enlarged over the role of government in the individualistic society. Counts's conception of the function of the school as a residual and a normative function clearly indicated that he stressed the interdependence and interrelatedness of social institutions and of man in society.

In discussing its abilities to secure limited social change, Counts urged more freedom for the school in determining policies to promote social betterment. However, the problem still remained as to the selection of the scale of values necessary to further this program of reconstruction. Counts found the particular problem complicated in the crucial areas of economics, politics, morals, and religion where diversity of opinion reigned and no one answer was accepted by all. The pluralism of American society aggravated this problem. In the last analysis, the forces dominant in society would plot the course.[9] This explains Counts's advocacy of the ascendancy of the laboring masses rather than of the forces motivated by the philosophy of economic individualism. Although Counts clearly outlined the magnitude of the problem relating to the normative function of the school, he did not precisely provide a means of resolving this problem. How would the conflicting groups in the pluralistic American society arrive at a framework of consensus as to the appropriate value criteria? Counts, himself, advocated a criterion that emphasized the ascendancy of collectivistic, cooperative, democratic, and scientific values. In reference to his proposed program of political action, apparently the acceptance of those collectivistic values would occur once the great masses of common people secured political control.

During the depression of the 1930s, Counts's analysis indicated that an economic aristocracy which controlled productive property dominated American life. He urged the inauguration of a collectivistic economy, the strengthening of the political sensibilities of the common people, and the revitalization of the equalitarian, democratic heritage to dislodge this dominant group and return control of social institutions and, hence, education to the common people. After securing this needed transformation of American society and a more comprehensive adjustment to the technological environment, he envisioned new social and educational horizons. Eventually, this reconstruction would culminate in a complete restoration of democracy in the United States.

Theoretical Reconstruction of Education

In *The Principles of Education,* Counts said that every age needed its own restatement of educational philosophy. Ra-

pidity of social change, advance of human thought, and changing conceptions of the worth of the individual human personality made any final formulation of educational philosophy
impossible. As social aims and values evolved, educational
aims, values, and purposes also evolved; objectives and methods required reconstruction with changing times.[10] Reconstruction of the theoretical foundations of life during a period of
profound change required special thought. Occupying a stra-
tegic location, education was necessarily at the very center of
the reconstructive process.[11] To cope with the crisis engendered by cultural transition and economic depression, Counts
urged the formulation of an educational philosophy adequate
to social demands. Representing great historic choices, this
philosophy needed substance as well as form. As an integral
part of civilization, the formulation of an educational program
was a creative act embracing analysis, selection, and synthesis.
It involved the making of choices among possibilities, affirma-
tion of values, and framing of individual and social purposes.
These decisions were conditioned by necessities of time and
circumstance. Both the social sciences and psychological disciplines aided the educational statesman in formulating such a
philosophy. The essential practical functions of these disciplines revealed the limits of choice and provided necessary
materials.[12] In a later section, the role of these disciplines in
the education of teachers will be pursued.

In the past, educators neglected the heart of the educational
problem. Most of their activity was superficial or confined to
sheer mechanics. They failed to deal with the central problem
of educational theory—the problem of relating education to
the nature and fortunes of American civilization.[13] The responses of educators to these problems will be explored in
greater depth later in this study. In restating the task, Counts
said that a great conception of education proceeded only from

a bold and creative confronting of the nature, values, conditions, and potentialities of civilization.[14]

Counts believed that the unemployment of the depression had eroded the traditional American faith in democratic processes and had induced a sense of widespread despair. He urged educators to identify with socially reconstructive forces and to come to grips with the problems caused by a society that lived in the midst of irreconcilable contradictions of affluence and poverty. Counts called for a profound social transformation that would lead Americans "from insecurity to security, from chaos to planning," from "private profit" to "collective security," and from "vulgar luxury and dire want" to a "shared abundant life." The major issue confronting both American society and education was that of controlling technological forces, processes, and products. Technology could continue to serve special interests or it could be used to advance the common good.[15]

Counts charged the educational profession with the positive task of creating a new tradition in American life. In urging the revitalizing of the American tradition, he suggested a vision of society which enriched and enobled the lives of the common people. Since the depression period had eroded the traditional faith in democracy, the age needed a great faith in which men could place their trust and pattern their aspirations. Counts believed that a reconstituted, revitalized philosophy and program of education exalting the democratic ethic could supply this needed faith.

The central part of the task of reconstruction of the educational philosophy of the United States was to apply the ideas, values, and outlooks of democracy to life and institutions. In order to accomplish this task, economic life was to be popularly controlled; the energies of technology released; special privilege and corruption eliminated; toleration, understanding and brotherhood promoted among races, peoples, and religions. The total national resources were to be mobilized against the forces of poverty and misery. Counts urged that knowledge be sought in all fields. But most of all, men were to positively engage in creating a civilization of justice, beauty, and worth.[16]

To assess the capabilities of the American system of education to meet the challenges which he outlined, Counts studied the potentialities and liabilities of the system. To understand more fully his efforts to secure a reconstructed philosophy and program of education, examination of Counts's analysis of the American educational system is necessary. After developing his civilizational approach to education, Counts turned to an analysis of the role of the school in American society. This study of Counts's social and educational theories is now directed to a consideration of the American educational tradition, the relationship of organized education to the problems of the depression, analysis of the curriculum, the responses made to educational problems, and finally to a proposed program for American education.

1. Counts, *Dare the School Build a New Social Order?* (New York: John Day Co., 1932), pp. 17–18.

2. Counts, *The Prospects of American Democracy* (New York: John Day Co., 1938), p. 357.

3. Crosby J. Chapman and George S. Counts, *Principles of Education* (Chicago: Houghton Mifflin Co., 1924), pp. 23–24.

4. Ibid., pp. 26–27.

5. John L. Childs, *American Pragmatism and Education* (New York: Henry Holt & Co., 1956), p. 241.

6. Counts, "The Place of the School in the Social Order," *National Education Association Proceedings*, 64 (1926), 310.

7. Chapman and Counts, pp. 46–47.

8. Herbert C. Espy, *The Public Secondary School: A Critical Analysis of Secondary Education in the United States* (Chicago: Houghton-Mifflin Co., 1939), p. 277.

9. Counts, "Place of the School," p. 313.

10. Chapman and Counts, p. 81.

11. George S. Counts, "The Meaning of a Liberal Education in Industrial Society," in the private library of George S. Counts, Carbondale, Illinois, p. 2.

12. Counts, *Prospects*, p. 318.

13. Counts, *Education and the Promise of America* (New York: Macmillan Co., 1946), p. 20.

14. Counts, *Education and American Civilization* (New York: Bureau of Publications, Teachers College, Columbia University, 1952), pp. 399–412.

15. "Educating for Tomorrow," *Social Frontier*, 1 (1934), 5.

16. Counts, *The Schools Can Teach Democracy* (New York: John Day Co., 1939), p. 13.

II. The American Educational Tradition

As Counts had examined the assets and liabilities of the American heritage, he also analyzed the potentialities of the American educational tradition to meet the challenges of cultural transition and economic dislocation. On the basis of his civilizational philosophy of education, Counts fashioned a program for American education. His careful consideration of the American educational tradition focused on the areas of: one, the immature American faith in the power of organized education; two, the impact of democratization and industrialization on the school; three, the local tradition of educational control; four, the status of educational opportunity; and five, the role of the American secondary school.

Immature American Faith in Education

In his published works, Counts criticized the traditional American faith in the power of formal education. Identifying the school with progress, Americans regarded education as life's unfailing solution to all problems. Since the founding of the Republic, American statesmen such as Washington, Franklin, Jefferson, and Madison preached enlightenment through schooling and insisted that the survival of free institutions required an educated citizenry.[1] To Counts, these early generations placed faith in the power of simple literacy in the belief that if men read then progress followed. Literate citizens, they believed, could control their own political destiny. Counts stated that the printed page had served as an instrument of deception as well as of enlightenment. Literacy facilitated the great campaigns of propaganda and chauvinism that led to international conflict and war.[2]

Counts discerned that during the period of the greatest expansion of organized education, world crises multiplied. Instead of directing social change, he found the school driven aimlessly by the forces transforming society.[3] This immature American faith in the power of the school derived from a notion of transcendence which regarded education as a pure and independent quality isolated from social, political, and economic conflict.[4] This uncritical notion inhibited serious, critical inquiries into the moral and social foundations of education. Although Americans associated education solely with democracy, subsequent historical events demonstrated that a popular form of education existed for every society or civilization. Counts found this traditional faith in education uncritical, immature, and naïve.

Having accepted the self-justification of education as something good in and of itself, Americans measured its advance in quantitative and physical terms. To Counts, this faith was further revealed by American willingness to support a costly and well-developed educational system. The growth of sec-

ondary school, college, and university enrollments and the
enormous study devoted to educational processes and methods
attested to the American faith in organized education.[5]

As Americans exalted their educational faith so did they
trust in the specialized educational institution of society, the
school. According to Counts, some educators, particularly progressives, erroneously conceived of the school as an all-powerful educational agency capable of reconstructing society without the intervention of other social institutions. By neglecting
the educative role of other social institutions, Counts felt these
educators assigned too powerful a role to the school. This, for
Counts, constituted a fundamental weakness of progressive
educational theory. As only one of several educative social institutions, the school had to maintain a constant awareness of
the changing functions and structures of the institutional order which determined its task. An educational theory based
solely upon events within the school lacked reality and vitality. To Counts, attempts to erect an educational theory upon
foundations which neglected institutional interdependence
would invariably prove timid, unimaginative, and inadequate.[6]

Americans also believed that formal education served only
democratic ends. Originating in the optimism generated by
the European Enlightenment, this belief carried over into the
American educational tradition. Formal education would enable man to constantly progress, and progress was translated
into democracy. Accepting the notion that education was intrinsically good, Americans took no definite means to insure
that education served democratic ends. As Counts had earlier
demonstrated, the very definition of democracy had become
confused. He pointed to the events which had transpired in
Russia, Germany, and Italy in the 1930s. These events graphically demonstrated that education could be deliberately or-

dered to serve any master, even a brutal and repressive one. In particular, Nazi Germany used organized education as a means of furthering racial hatred, violence, and an irrational chauvinism. These undemocratic and irrational uses of education demonstrated the validity of Counts's assertion that education served the dominant forces in society. They further revealed the shallowness of the American faith that conceived of education as always intrinsically good, progressive, and democratic.

In 1930, Counts stated that Americans attributed such power to organized education that the school served as the American road to culture. His depression period works, *The Social Foundations of Education,* 1934, and *The Prospects of American Democracy,* 1938, criticized this immature faith in education. *Education and the Promise of America,* 1946, *Education and American Civilization,* 1952, and *The Foundations of Human Freedom,* 1962, continued to challenge this tradition. Although Counts was apparently justified in condemning this simple American faith in education since it isolated the school from society, some lack of faith must have existed in the minds of many Americans. During the depression period, demands urging retrenchment of educational expenditures were accepted to the detriment of the school program. Unless some shadow of doubt existed, these demands would not have achieved the success which they experienced.

Education and Industrial America

After treating the American faith in education, Counts discussed the growth of organized education in America. In preindustrial America, the task of inducting the child into

group life resided primarily in the family, neighborhood, and
community. Ordinary economic and social obligations did not
require proficiency in reading, writing, and arithmetic. Among
the common people, boys performed manual arts and girls
practiced domestic skills under parental tutelage. As the child
matured, he acquired occupational skills and knowledge appropriate to his station in life. At this informal level, Counts
stated education possessed an intimate connection with life
and served as a source of civic and moral training.[7] The family
was not the only educational agency in preindustrial society.
The farming community, rural neighborhood, church, press,
and district school also constituted genuine social and educative forces.

Counts stated that the industrial revolution altered these
patterns of familial education. As industrialization weakened
the inherited, informal educational agencies, the magnitude of
the educational task and the program of the school increased
in scope, size, and complexity. An interrelated society, evolved
by industrialization, involved the individual in affairs beyond
his immediate level of experience. Thus, the task of inducting
the child into the great world complex bore little resemblance
to the task of preparing the individual for life in the now outmoded, preindustrial, agrarian community.[8] Increased discoveries and inventions required the transmission of a large and
complex body of knowledge which was fundamental to the
operations of industrialized society. Science and technology
had produced a dependency on modes and systems of thought
which could be mastered only by rigorous application and
study.[9]

Counts stated that social change influenced the course of
organized education. Following a period of brutalizing child
labor, political reformers reduced the role of the child in manu-

facturing through child labor laws. Coinciding with the re-
strictions on child labor, the enactment of compulsory school
attendance laws occurred. Increasingly children reached maturity without engaging in socially useful labor. Although
educational opportunity increased, the intimate connections
between learning and daily life were reduced by the growing
complexity of the industrialized social order.

Influence of Economic Individualism on Education

As noted in Counts's discussion of the middle class ascendancy in American political, social, and economic life, this class
also dominated education in post–Industrial Revolution America. An alliance between businessman and educator characterized American educational history. Under the leadership of
Barnard and Harris, American schools supplied the factories
and mills of industrialized America with contented and docile
laborers. Public education profited greatly from the advance
of industrialization in America and tax monies marked for
educational expenditure increased. Counts found that the financial support of private enterprise increased the period of
schooling and also the number of enrollments in elementary,
secondary, and higher institutions. It also contributed to increased expenditures for school buildings and physical equipment. New educational enterprises were launched under the
spell that the American people were on the threshold of the
realization of the equalization of educational opportunities.
The American economy, swollen by private enterprise, provided large financial support for the physical advance of public
education in the United States.[10]

As the educational enterprise profited from the alliance with private enterprise, the school accepted the individualistic philosophy of the dominant middle class business group and supported the ideals of protection of private property, enforcement of contracts, and perpetuation of the free market.[11] Counts found that much of the school program was based on the principle of encouraging the individual to compete with his fellows in the struggle for admission into the privileged class. The great mass of the American people, he said, viewed organized education as a ladder reaching to preferred financial, occupational, and social status.[12]

As he continued his analysis of the origins of public education in the United States, Counts found that at the base of educational theory rested a profound faith in the potentialities of individual men. Unfortunately this faith was clouded by the same confusion which beset individualism in other areas of life. The Jeffersonian concept of personal freedom had been confused with the doctrines of laissez faire individualism. Although the advocates of economic individualism shouted the old agrarian slogans, their peculiar brand of individualism produced the demise of individual opportunity. Nevertheless, the principle of individual success greatly influenced American education.

Counts's analysis of American society during the depression of the 1930s revealed the necessity of a collective economic order of life. If deliberate and planful controls were not exercised over technological forces, Counts feared that continued economic anarchy would characterize American life. Unfortunately, the alliance of educator and businessman prevented the school from educating for the emergent collectivistic age. Almost everywhere the school, controlled by reactionary forces, perpetuated obsolete ideas inherited from the philosophy of economic individualism.[13]

Finally, Counts charged the capitalistic system with isolating the school from life. This isolation erected an artificial barrier between public and private interest. Although sound education intimately connected school and society, vested economic interests demanded that the school ignore social problems which threatened the status quo. He asserted that as long as private profit motivated social life, the school was destined to dwell in an artificial world.[14] Isolated from society, public education revealed little comprehension of the character of industrial civilization. Although responsible for the teaching of science, organized education ignored the scientific method. Although transmitting the words of the American historic tradition, the educational program neglected genuinely democratic values. Instead, organized education fostered egoistic and competitive values suited to an obsolete society. He found that the American system of public education failed to effectively encourage needed social and cooperative values. The laissez faire tradition of economic individualism postulated that man was naturally competitive. According to this competitive philosophy, excellence was motivated by egocentric rather than socially directed impulses. Contending that social institutions were effective only as they stimulated competition for favored positions in society, the American educational system conceived of the nation as a living monument to individual enterprise.[15]

According to Counts, the major attraction of school attendance was the promise of future financial reward. This prevalent assumption, which judged public education in monetary terms, revealed the extent to which the pecuniary ideal of individualized success dominated educational theory. In terms of social philosophy, economic individualism conceived the general welfare best served by the pursuit of selfish interest.

Within the school, motivation rested primarily on appeals to individual self-interest. To stimulate achievement, an elaborate system of marks, credits, and degrees at every educational level evolved. Although various forms of socialized activity were slowly introduced under the impetus of progressive education, the school relationship still resembled that of a contract between pupil and teacher.[16]

According to the analysis provided by Counts in *The American Road to Culture* and *The Social Foundations of Education,* the philosophy and program of American education was ill-suited to meet the problems of cultural transition and economic depression. An alliance between educator and businessman sapped the vitality of organized education and perpetuated a status quo based upon economic individualism. Unless needed reconstruction of educational philosophy proceeded, the future of democracy seemed dark for Counts as he analyzed the nation's educational enterprise during the depression period.

The American Educational Structure

After analyzing the immature faith of Americans in education and the domination of organized education by business groups, Counts discussed the administration of the American school system. Patterns of public school organization were largely derived from the experiences of the westward movement. In stressing the frontier influence on patterns of American settlement, Counts pointed to the distrust of legal authorities, especially that of the federal government. This attitude toward government, combined with the New England pattern of organization of town or district school, influenced the positing of educational control at the most immediate level, the local school board. In patterns of administration and organization, American education reflected the agrarian-frontier tradition while the pursuit of mechanical efficiency in its program reflected the industrial-business civilization. To Counts, this strange union of practices led to an incongruous mixture of agrarian and industrial, rural and urban, in the administration of American education.[17]

Counts found the local control tradition of the common school derived from patterns of settlement, as the administration of public functions devolved upon local communities. School boundaries were fixed by the practical concerns of topography, transportation, birth rate, material resources, level of cultural standards, and the prevailing concept of educational needs. This pattern of organization resulted in the one room district school so long present on the American scene.[18] Placing their faith in extreme forms of local initiative in educational affairs, the local community, rather than the state or federal government, exercised the dominant role in control, support, and conduct of public education. The decenetralization of the American system of public education was supposed to bring the school into intimate contact with the people. According to this homespun theory, the boards of education, elected on the local district level, were to arouse popular interest in the schools and make education sensitive to popular demands. Contrary to this theoretical expectation, Counts found that after the passing of the agrarian age, vested interest groups dominated education.

The policies of decentralization, encouraging local initiative and respect for private enterprise, produced institutional autonomy. With no provision for unified coordination, each local educational unit zealously guarded its autonomy. This pattern produced needless duplication of effort and generally failed to articulate a social philosophy for education. The jealous autonomy, pride, and inefficient machinery that resulted from local control made it extremely difficult to introduce quickly and effectively into the school the tested results of educational science. Acting as a conservative control, it also made it virtually impossible to achieve sudden and sweeping changes in the educational program.[19]

During the depression years of the 1930s, Counts urged the school to undertake the building of a new social order, meet the needs of emerging technological civilization, and preserve democracy during a time of transition and economic crisis. His analysis of the school with its strong tradition of local initiative and autonomy indicated that the existing educational system would be a reluctant if not impossible vehicle for action in the reconstruction of a durable educational philosophy and program. Rather than rely on the cumbersome educational apparatus to achieve needed reform, Counts directed appeals instead to the educational profession. This call to the educational profession, the teachers of the nation, will be discussed later.

As a result of local control, the school reflected the vices as well as the virtues of the American people. The school exhibited the cultural limitations of the dominant forces controlling local education. The intellectual classes, often with limited economic power, had little impact on the conduct of public education. At times, education reflected the popular, but often irrational, prejudices and biases of the public's passions. As an example of these prejudices, Counts called attention to the prohibition of German studies during World War I, the extreme Anglophobe tendencies exhibited by Mayor Thompson of Chicago in his purges of educators, and the barring of the teaching of evolution by legislative enactment in Tennessee resulting in the famed Scopes Trial of 1925.

In his analysis of the evolution of American public education, Counts discussed the relatively minor role exercised by the federal government throughout much of the nation's history. The inherited pattern of local control, based on the New England school district, became the prevalent pattern of educational organization throughout most of the United States. Many Americans were fearful of placing too much authority in the hands of the federal government and believed it a wiser course to diffuse educational powers. Accordingly, the United States Constitution reserved education to the states, which in turn delegated large amounts of authority to the local districts. When the inherited tradition of local school control was combined with the philosophy of laissez faire economic individualism, federal involvement in the guarded area of local education was ruled out and regarded as an encroachment on state and local sovereignty. Counts believed that the inherited patterns of decentralized, local school authorities were inadequate to initiate the changes needed to cope with the problems of a massive urban and technological society.

Dominant Classes Control Boards of Education

In the preceding discussion, Counts was found to assert that a philosophy based upon laissez faire individualism dominated American education. In addition to this philosophic orientation, the local school districts, resistant of centralized authority, became the prevalent pattern of educational control. The factors of individualism and local control contributed to the positing of educational control in the hands of the powerful

business and professional groups which dominated community life. In 1927, Counts examined the domination of boards
of education by such groups in his study *The Social Composition of Boards of Education,* a monograph that produced
considerable controversy at the time of its publication.

In *The Social Composition of Boards of Education,* Counts
wrote that public education reflected the domination of powerful social classes which controlled boards of education. He
found the teacher merely a creature who was forced to con-
form to the standards of the board of education. The content,
spirit, and purpose of public education reflected the biases, limitations, and experiences of the board members. In surveying
representative boards of education throughout the United
States, Counts divided the members into seven major occupational categories: proprietors, professionals, managerial, commercial, clerical, manual laborers, and agriculturalists.[21] He
concluded that boards of education were drawn predominantly
from the favored classes of merchants, lawyers, manufacturers,
bankers, and doctors of the first two categories listed above.
Few members were chosen from the less favored clerical, manual, and agricultural occupations.[22]

Because of the favored positions of these classes which dominated school boards, Counts found them conservative or resistant to social change. This conservative bias was reflected
in the prevailing characteristics of school systems. Counts assumed without question the soundness of the assertion that
genuine conflicts of interest existed between the various economic classes in society. He stated that the members of one
economic class could scarcely be expected to protect the interests of other classes.[23] Once again, he stressed the importance of economic conditioning in shaping social philosophy
and in fixing the group loyalties in the conflicts characterizing

modern society. A dominant class, he said, was a privileged class favored by the existing social arrangements. It tended to be conservative, to exaggerate the merits of the status quo, and to fear social change. Counts concluded, as long as the school was controlled by the dominant class it would be oriented to the past and be defensive and conservative rather than creative and progressive:

> The argument may be advanced that these board members, though drawn from a restricted class, will, because of the superior educational opportunities which they have enjoyed, rise above a narrow loyalty to their own group and formulate educational policies in terms of the common interest. We all wish that this were so, but there is little evidence from the human past to support it. The rare individual will strive earnestly to have regard for the best interests of all classes, but no one can transcend the limits set by his own experience. The best of us are warped and biased by the very process of living.[24]

Counts's work of 1927 inaugurated a very significant trend in educational research and theory related to the social implications of education. He asserted that education was dominated by favored socio-economic groups. Many theorists since that time have begun their research with an acceptance of Counts's conclusions.

Counts's assumptions regarding the domination of education by favored classes were challenged by W. W. Charters in the article, "Social Class Analysis and the Control of Public Education." Although Charters accepted the contention that business and professional persons from the upper middle class of the community were numerically preponderant on boards of education, he questioned three other assertions that Counts made: one, that these professional and business classes were more conservative than the lower economic classes; two, that social class determined educational bias; and three, that the values of the dominant class entered into the decision-making process.[25]

Charters alleged that Counts's conclusions were based on insufficient evidence. Charters contended that professional men were more progressive than any other occupational group represented on school boards while clerical workers were among the least progressive. Charters stated that two other possible conclusions other than those suggested by Counts were possible: one, wealthy and professional men did not reflect conservative class values; two, they reflected dominant class values but these were not conservative.[26] Charters did not explain his use of the words progressive and conservative. For Counts, these words indicated a propensity for or against directed social change. Charters might have sharpened his criticism by indicating whether his use of the terms progressive and conservative applied to the introduction of innovations into the school program or whether they referred to a willingness to advance social change through the school. Both the conclusions of Charters and Counts would have been more precise had they applied the meanings given to conservative and progressive to definite school policies and programs.

Charters further stated that the evidence available failed to indicate a clear relationship between the policy stands taken by school board members and their social class positions in the community. He found it entirely possible that a man who became a school board official spoke and voted differently from the way he did as a private citizen. He stated that the social role of a responsible public officer imposed obligations far different from those imposed upon the anonymous community citizen. Further, those selected as board members might hold a wider set of values than those of narrow class interests. Charters also questioned that a person classified as occupying a particular social class position would internalize the values associated with that position. Members of a social class group, he said, did not always adhere to the values and norms appropriate to their group relationships.[27]

Charters suggested that the entire area of social class and school policy needed further study and research based on modern sociological methodology. Although Counts's interpretation had influenced a generation of educational theorists, it might be said that the interpretation was over-generalized. Both Counts and Charters needed a more precise definition of the meanings of conservative and progressive in regard to school board membership policy-making.

Single Track American Educational System

Despite the prevailing patterns of local and business control of the educational system, Counts attributed great significance to the emergence in American public education of the single track educational system, the "educational ladder." This distinctly American pattern of education repudiated aristocratic European institutions and established the principle of a single educational system for all of the American people. In light of his emphasis on equalitarianism as a basic constituent of American democracy, Counts regarded the "educational ladder" as a strong support for the continuance of equality.

According to Counts's analysis of the single-track American system of education, elementary school, secondary school, and the state college and university constituted a continuous program of publicly supported education from childhood to professional and graduate study. These publicly supported and controlled institutions provided educational opportunity to all who met the modest scholastic requirements.[28] Despite the increasing economic stratification of the depression period, the "educational ladder" existed as the safest guarantee against the rigid social stratification characteristic of Europe. He termed the sequential organization of the "educational ladder" the most magnificent achievement of American democracy in the educational area.[29] The key to the establishment of the "educational ladder" rested, according to Counts, in the founding of the American public high school. As an upward extension of the elementary system, the secondary school transformed the dual educational system into a single, unified system. The American public high school, which enjoyed phenomenal growth at the turn of the twentieth century, gave concrete expression to the principle of equality of educational opportunity.[30] The growth of the high school, in turn, made possible the extension of the state colleges and universities to the masses of people. The unification of the elementary school, through the secondary school, to the college facilitated the upward surge of the masses to higher levels of educational achievement. Although still motivated essentially by a desire for individual and financial success, this upward educational movement constituted a profound social movement.[31]

Despite Counts's enthusiasm for the comprehensive high school, this educational institution was in reality a multi-track system. The various specialized curricula such as the commercial, the vocational, and college preparatory tended to divide students along lines of their future occupation. As Counts pointed out, these occupational preferences were often determined by parental occupation. Despite this obvious shortcoming, the comprehensive high school was still a significant achievement of democratic education for two reasons: one, as an upward extension of the public elementary school it brought students from all social classes, races, and religions into contact; two, it provided publicly supported and controlled secondary education to all students desiring it.

Counts further cautioned that in the final analysis America still lacked a completely integrated educational system. Although not a part of the public educational system, Counts did not specifically criticize the parochial schools maintained by religious sects as violating the single track principle. Since tuition charges were low and the student population representative of the general population, the Roman Catholic and other religious schools had much the same social composition as the public schools. However, certain primary, secondary, and higher schools, catering to privileged families, were regarded as class institutions which perpetuated the "economic aristocracy." [32] In addition, a dual system of education existed in the former slave states of the American South. Adhering to canons of rigid racial segregation, two parallel systems existed in the South—one for whites and the other for Negroes. Although supposedy separate but equal, the Negro schools were generally inferior, inadequately supported, and confined largely to the primary level. As early as 1930, Counts stated that even if conditions were completely equalized, the dual system constituted a denial of the principle of educational equality to the Negro.

Counts's analysis of the single-track educational system indicated that it constituted an important force in maintaining social mobility and equality of opportunity despite certain imperfections. It could serve significantly in furthering a comprehensive educational program designed to aid in solving the problems of cultural transition and economic dislocation. If a comprehensive and truly democratic educational philosophy and program were formulated, the "educational ladder" might aid in checking the domination by an "economic aristocracy."

Equality of Educational Opportunity

After his survey of the single-track educational system of the United States, Counts focused attention on a matter of deep concern, the realization of equality of educational opportunity. In his analysis of the origins of American democracy, Counts stressed the factor of economic equality as a conditioning force in bringing about social and political equality. This condition of economic, social, and political equality produced American democracy. During the 1930s, the rise of economic inequality gave rise to an "economic aristocracy." As a result, democracy was jeopardized. To decrease the tendency to aristocracy, education could exercise a vital role by making educational opportunity available to all. Although the "educational ladder" fulfilled a tremendous function in securing educational opportunity, much of this vaunted opportunity was sheerly theoretical and did not reach the practical and immediate levels.

Counts found that inequality of educational opportunity persisted in the United States. While class and other forms of discrimination prevailed, the vestiges of the European dual system of education remained. In the private schools, traditions of class rule, privilege, and superiority continued. In the private preparatory and secondary schools which prepared students for entry into the highly restricted and selective colleges, class rule in education was perpetuated. Counts asserted that it was to these institutions that families of entrenched social and economic status sent their children.[33] Within the private schools and colleges maintained by the "economic aristocracy," an education designed to train a ruling elite in their functions as rulers existed. Counts found such a system of education incompatible with genuine democracy and equality of opportunity.

In addition to the class consciousness of certain educational institutions, Counts also condemned racial discrimination. The principles of educational opportunity were not applied to certain racial and cultural minorities. Indians, Jews, Orientals and members of recently arrived minorities encountered discrimination which blocked entrance into the professions. As mentioned, Counts severely criticized the prolonged, severe, and general discrimination inflicted on the American Negro throughout the nation and particularly in the dual educational system of the South.[34]

The highly esteemed local system of educational control also perpetuated inequality of educational opportunity since the ability to support educational institutions varied greatly from state to state, and from locality to locality. Great diversity existed in educational expenditures per pupil from state to state. This diversity caused some American children, especially in rural areas and in the South, to receive an education inferior to that offered in the highly industrialized urban areas of some northern states.[35]

As Counts wrote in the 1930s, the effects of the depression were being felt in demands for retrenchment of educational expenditures. Reduction of teachers' salaries, outlays for school buildings, and needed educational services occurred as the antiquated local tax structures were unable to support public education in many areas. In addition, sources of revenue were depleted as productive capacity and earning power decreased in the wake of rising unemployment. The old allies of the educator, businessmen, led the demands for educational retrenchment. Counts stated that when cultural services were reduced during periods of economic depression the shock fell unevenly on the different classes in the different localities. While the educational opportunities of the wealthy remained unimpaired, those of the less favored groups were greatly curtailed.[36] Depression-produced poverty was a great factor in reducing equality of educational opportunity.

In view of Counts's analysis of the necessity of equality of opportunity in a democratic society, maintenance of educational opportunity was a serious concern. Fearful of perpetuation of the "economic aristocracy," Counts sought ways to curtail inequality of educational opportunity. As he relied on the efficacy of informed political action, he also trusted to a limited degree in the power of education to maintain democratic processes. Although American education lacked the philosophy and program needed to reverse inequality, it contained the embryonic machinery necessary for a reconstruction of the American social order along equalitarian, collectivistic, and thoroughly democratic lines.

Growth of the American Secondary School

In his discussion of the "educational ladder," Counts called attention to the American secondary school as the institution which linked the public elementary school and the state university. Much of his writing before the depression analyzed the role of the high school in the American educational system.

Although essentially statistical studies, his works, *The Selective Character of American Secondary Education,* 1922, and *The Senior High School Curriculum,* 1926, demonstrated Counts's interest in investigating the social implications of secondary education. *Secondary Education and Industrialism,* 1929, indicated his continued interest in the relationships of the American high school to the major currents of American society.

Counts directed attention to the phenomenal growth enjoyed by the American secondary school since the turn of the century. Although in 1891 only 300,000 students enrolled in public secondary schools, thirty-eight years later in 1929 the number had reached almost 5,000,000.[37] Attendance at secondary school, no longer a rare privilege, was enjoyed by half of the nation's adolescents.

In *The American Road to Culture,* Counts defined the typical American secondary school as an institution embracing the entire range of subjects and enrolling students from diverse cultural and vocational backgrounds. While the organization of separate secondary institutions for industrial, commercial, and traditional academic subjects would segregate the adolescent population into distinct occupational groups and accentuate socio-economic differences, the American comprehensive high school brought students together. Regardless of occupational destination, the comprehensive high school prolonged the period of common schooling and association provided by the public elementary school. To Counts, the comprehensive high school, a product of democracy, promoted social mobility and demonstrated the willingness of all groups to live in a common society.[38]

After noting the rapid increase in publicly supported secondary education and defining the nature of the comprehen-

sive high school, Counts analyzed the social and economic
conditions which accelerated the growth of the high school in
the United States. Once again, the growth of the secondary
school reflected the social, political, and economic conditions
prevalent in a given society at a definite historical period. According to Counts, the democratization of the secondary school
proceeded from the existence of certain social ideals in the
United States, the prior extension of elementary education, the
appearance of a highly integrated society within the framework
of a complex civilization, and finally the increase in national
wealth, and the decline of the birth and death rates.[39]

The combined forces of democratization and industrialization shattered the traditional molds of American secondary education. The late nineteenth century witnessed the demise of
the Latin Grammar school as the secondary school of the selected few. Although at mid-century the academy had experienced a flourish of growth, the educational ladder was still incomplete. Increasingly, the upward extension of democracy in
education reached the secondary level. In addition, business
leaders demanded trained laborers in various mechanical and
clerical skills. These democratic and industrial pressures promoted educational experimentation and innovation. Counts
asserted that the conception of secondary education for the
privileged gradually succumbed to the assaults of political democracy and the increased demands of a society of growing
complexity and wealth.[40] The growth of the publicly supported secondary school coincided with the period of political
reformation in American history characterized by the Populist
and Progressive Movements. Social ideals emerged to the effect
that the individual should be judged in terms of inherent
worth and permitted to achieve any station in society commensurate with his talents, efforts, and character.[41]

To Counts, the extension of the elementary school eventually produced the growth of the secondary school. Stating that the really creative period in the development of the elementary school occurred in the second and third quarters of the nineteenth century, he termed this achievement a necessary foundation for the subsequent growth of the secondary school. Since the secondary school was an upward extension of the elementary school, the expansion of the high school proceeded only when elementary education was well advanced.[42] As the growth of elementary education had been an achievement of agrarian society, the expansion of the secondary school was a creation of industrial society. Before the industrialization of the United States, only a selected few had received a secondary education. Counts elaborated on the connections between industrialism and the growth of the high school:

> On the one hand, regions, groups, and individuals specialize increasingly and become more and more dependent upon each other and upon the whole; and, on the other, the evolution of the means of transportation and communication provides the instruments of this specialization and interdependence. If we take the spread of these inventions as an index of the increasing integration of society, we shall find that it has proceeded pari passu with the expansion of the high school.[43]

The integration of industrial society required a widening of the intellectual and social capacities of individuals. As the individual was inducted into the large society which he knew only indirectly and from a distance, he depended less on immediate and unorganized personal experience and more on the formal agencies of education. The increasing integration of

society wrought by industrialism opened up individual opportunities of a most diverse kind. Because of increased mobility,
the individual was no longer confined to the narrow and limited geographical and social circle of his birth. Not only did
increased mobility introduce the individual to new and varied
situations, it also made increased secondary education practical. Counts stated that whereas attendance at secondary
school was theoretically possible earlier, the development of
rapid transportation in a relatively thinly populated country
made high school attendance practically possible. Increased
mobility made attendance at high schools geographically feasi-
ble.[44]

Finally, industrialization produced the wealth needed to
finance increased educational expenditures for secondary
school support. A declining birth rate and extension of the life
span produced changes in the ratio of children to adults. As
the number of adults increased, economic burdens lifted from
children. These forces made attendance at school possible for
a longer period of time and resulted in increased secondary
school enrollments.[45]

Selective Character of American Secondary Education

As indicated in the foregoing discussion, the growth of the
American secondary school characterized an expansive democratic and industrial society. However, in *The Selective Character of American Secondary Education,* 1922, Counts indicated that the high school failed in fulfilling the democratic
aspirations of many proponents of a common, publicly supported educational system. Although the public high school
existed in almost every community, Counts stated that the

American high school retained a selective character. Despite the rapid increase in enrollment since 1890, high school students were still a highly selected group. Counts concluded that secondary education was still not education for adolescence but rather education for a selected group of adolescents.[46]

Although the title of Counts's work seemed to imply that the American high school selected its student population on the basis of socio-economic class, this was not the case. The school did not perform the task of selecting some students and rejecting others on the basis of class. While social and economic conditions made it possible for some students to attend high school, these conditions also made it difficult for others to attend. Thus, students from the less favored classes were not rejected by the school but rather by the economic conditions prevailing in society. It might be stated, then, that the element of selectivity resided informally within society rather than within the framework of the secondary school.

By conducting a statistical survey of a number of high schools, Counts concluded that the secondary school essentially served the upper social strata in the population. He discovered a close correlation between parental occupation and high school attendance. According to numbers of students enrolled, Counts established the following occupation rankings: professionals, businessmen, commercial service, and common laborers. The order of the number of students enrolled reflected the social and economic status of the occupation, its educational and intellectual standards, and the stability of employment.[47] Counts was convinced that those groups poorly represented numerically in the high school patronized the more narrow and practical curricula which served as a terminus in the educational system and prepared for wage earning. These one or two year vocational courses chiefly drew registration from the children of the poorly represented laborers. Therefore, Counts concluded, parental occupation, as one index of cultural level, exhibited a close correlation to educational opportunity.[48] Also, more children of native stock attended high school than the less favored children of recent immigrant parentage. The numbers of Negro children enrolled in high school was much less than the total proportion of Negroes to the whole population.

Counts concluded that the high school education was being extended at public expense to those very classes that already occupied the favored positions in modern society. This misuse of the secondary school aided the forces which perpetuated social inequality. Publicly supported secondary education could be justified only in terms of the unqualified recognition on the part of the high school student of the social obligation involved.[49]

As earlier indicated, Counts found control of the secondary school vested in the favored classes dominating American society. These dominant classes controlled boards of education and determined programs and policies. Except where the farmer retained control, educational control rested with the capitalistic and associated classes.[50] These classes which controlled the secondary school were the same groups which had the largest enrollments in the nation's high schools.

Recommendation of Universal High School Education

Since secondary education was so important in completing the single-track educational system, Counts suggested formulation of the objectives of secondary education in terms of social demands. Although there had been some expansion of the high school curriculum, secondary education had failed to respond to the needs of American civilization. Through association with the traditional curriculum, new subjects quickly lost vitality and imitated the outmoded characteristics of the older materials of instruction.[51]

Counts found that the theoretical ideal of equality of educational opportunity did not guarantee equal opportunities. Instead of reliance on a selective criteria of birth or social position, Counts demanded the recognition of the potentialities of each individual student without reference to caste or class. He urged high school administrators to subscribe to an open enrollment policy or to publicly restrict secondary education to all but a selected group. However, if the principle of selection continued, he urged that objective methods of selection be used and that the selected group of students be taught the meaning of social obligation.[52]

Counts realized that the implementation of his suggestions for the equalization of secondary education opportunities was limited by the forces that controlled education. These groups tended to conserve the existent system rather than to promote change in the social order. The dominant forces controlling the secondary school and American education represented the values of the past rather than the future. These forces used the school as an instrument to either prevent social change or to serve their own special purposes. Unless new methods of controlling the school evolved or unless the educational profession was given a freer hand in determining policies, the school could not be expected to become a creative social agent.[53] Forced to operate within the confines of the existing system, the transformation of the American secondary school could proceed only with great difficulty.

Although high school enrollments in the 1920s and 1930s

were dominated by students from the upper social classes, Counts believed that the tendency of industrialization would be to reduce such social selectivity in the educational sphere. Industrialization would increase the need for additional skills and knowledge, and secondary school attendance would extend to the lower economic groups. He asserted:

> Any defensible or sound theory of secondary education must be in essential harmony with the great social trends which characterize the age. So it is in this matter of selection. We might all wish to bring back the highly selective secondary school of history, but industrial society had decreed otherwise.[54]

Counts's early statistical works, *The Selective Character of American Secondary Education* (1922) and *The Senior High School Curriculum* (1926), had stressed the high degree of selectivity of the students attending secondary school. However, by the time of his work of 1929, *Secondary Education and Industrialism,* the democratic and industrial forces that had initially caused the high school expansion continued to erode the selective characteristics of the high school. The evolution of the high school resembled the earlier evolution of the elementary school. As compulsory elementary school attendance laws had universalized elementary education, compulsory school age requirements had weakened the selective character of the high school. The American high school experienced many of the same patterns of growth experienced earlier by the elementary school.

Counts's works on the secondary school were significant in the history of educational research. They also indicated some of the trends that were to be developed more fully in his more general educational writings. They revealed a gradual change in emphasis from statistical studies of certain restricted educational problems to the more general issue of education as a part of American civilization. In these later works, Counts applied his theory of the relationships between civilization and education. By the 1930's, Counts advanced his research from the study of limited educational problems to a comprehensive analysis of American civilization and the formulation of an over-all philosophy and program of education.

Summation of Counts's Analysis

Counts's treatment of the American educational tradition revealed certain obvious strengths and weaknesses in the proposal that the school be used to advance a program of social reconstruction. The fact that the American people accepted publicly supported education was an asset that favored the use of the school as a reconstructive agency. On the other hand, there existed such obvious liabilities in the educational tradition as, one, continued inequality of education; two, local control in the hands of vested interest groups intent on preserving the status quo; three, the selective character of much of secondary education. In the face of these detriments to social reconstruction through the existing educational machinery, Counts addressed his pleas to the teaching profession rather than to those who controlled the school.

Counts's *The American Road to Culture* (1930) represented a contribution to the history of American education. Rather than being a highly documented work, this highly interpretive study was an introduction to the more analytical

The Social Foundations of Education (1934) and to the more polemical *The Prospects of American Democracy* (1938). Much of Counts's interpretation of American educational history accepted the traditional viewpoints, with the exception that he stressed industrialization and class consciousness as factors in educational control. After examining the American educational past, Counts turned to some of the specific responses made by various educational theorists to the problems of the 1930s.

1. George S. Counts, *Education and the Promise of America* (New York: Macmillan Co., 1946), p. 17.

2. Counts, *The Social Foundations of Education* (New York: Charles Scribner's Sons, 1934), p. 533.

3. Counts, "Education For What?" *New Republic,* 71 (1935), 12.

4. Counts, *The American Road to Culture* (New York: John Day Co., 1930), p. 184.

5. Ibid., p. 17.

6. Ibid., p. 18.

7. Counts, *Social Foundations,* p. 255.

8. Ibid., p. 258.

9. Ibid., p. 259.

10. Counts, "Business and Education," *Teachers College Record,* 39 (1938), 556.

11. Counts, "Presentday Reasons for Requiring a Longer Period of Pre-Service Preparation for Teachers," *National Education Association Proceedings,* 73 (1935), 698.

12. Counts, *Social Foundations,* pp. 519–20.

13. Counts, "Education For What?," p. 12.

14. Committee of the Progressive Education Association on Social and Economic Problems, *A Call to the Teachers of the Nation* (New York: John Day Co., 1933), p. 23.

15. Counts, *American Road,* p. 76.

16. Ibid., pp. 71–72.

17. Counts, *Social Foundations,* p. 267.

18. Ibid.

19. Counts, *American Road,* pp. 56–57.

20. Ibid., pp. 51–52.

21. Counts, *The Social Composition of Boards of Education* (Chicago: University of Chicago Press, 1927), p. 51.

22. Ibid., p. 83.

23. Ibid., p. 4.

24. Ibid., p. 90.

25. W. W. Charters, "Social Class Analysis and the Control of Public Education," *The Sociology of Education,* ed. Robert R. Bell, (Homewood, Ill.: Dorsey Press, 1962), pp. 176–77.

26. Ibid., p. 178.

27. Ibid., p. 181.

28. Ibid., p. 65.

29. Ibid., p. 79.

30. Counts, *The Senior High School Curriculum* (Chicago: University of Chicago Press, 1926), p. 1.

31. Counts, *American Road,* pp. 66–67.

32. Ibid., pp. 80–81.

33. Counts, *Social Foundations,* p. 263.

34. Ibid., pp. 264–65.

35. Ibid., p. 266.

36. Ibid.

37. Counts, "Selection as a Function of American Secondary Education," *National Education Association Proceedings,* 67 (1929), 596.

38. Counts, *American Road,* pp. 85–86.

39. Counts, *Secondary Education and Industrialism* (Cambridge, Mass.: Harvard University Press, 1929), pp. 23–24.

40. Counts, *The Selective Character of American Secondary Education* (Chicago: University of Chicago Press, 1922), p. 3.

41. Counts, *Secondary Education and Industrialism*, p. 25.

42. Counts, "Selection as a Function," 598.

43. Ibid.

44. Ibid.

45. Ibid., 601–2.

46. Counts, *Selective Character*, p. 141.

47. Ibid., pp. 141–42.

48. Ibid., pp. 142–43.

49. Ibid., p. 152.

50. Counts, "The Place of the School in the Social Order," *National Education Association Proceedings*, 64 (1926), 313.

51. Counts, *Senior High School Curriculum*, p. 146.

52. Counts, *Selective Character*, p. 156.

53. Counts, "Place of the School," pp. 314–15.

54. Counts, "Selection as a Function," p. 602.

III. Educational Responses to the 1930s

Counts examined some of the major educational responses to the problems of the 1930s. In addition to formulating his own educational philosophy of democratic collectivism, he discussed four other educational responses: education as purely intellectual; education as essential subject matter; education as a science; and finally, education as viewed by Progressives. This chapter will consider first Counts's attitudes to educational responses outside of the progressive community and then turn more fully to a discussion of Counts's relations to progressive thought during the 1930s.

During the 1930s, Counts took issue with three educational theories that existed outside of the progressive matrix. Two of these, purely intellectual education and essentialist education for adjustment to the existent social order, were completely outside of the experimentalist climate which characterized progressivism. The third theory, the scientific movement in education, occupied an intermediate position. Emphasizing educational efficiency, the scientific movement served conservative educational practice and also stressed the nature of the child and the laws of learning as did progressive education.

Education as Purely Intellectual

For Counts, education was not exclusively intellectual, nor merely a process of acquiring facts and ideas. The major function of education was the induction of the immature into group life. This function involved not only development of intellectual powers, but also character formation, acquisition of habits, attitudes, and dispositions suited to specific living conditions, a given cultural level, and a definite body of ideals and aspirations.[1] In *Dare the School Build a New Social Order?*, Counts attacked the advocates of a purely intellectual educational philosophy. From his point of view, purely intellectual education produced agnostic individuals detached from social realities and issues. He condemned such persons who, while seeing all sides to every question, committed themselves to none.[2]

In particular, Counts rejected the theory of Robert M. Hutchins, author of *The Higher Learning in America* (1936), which advocated an educational program based upon the study of the great classics of Western civilization. Counts, like Dewey, found Hutchins's theory to be totally inadequate to pressing social needs. Counts called the Hutchins theory a manifestation of academic nostalgia for the days of classical learning long since passed. Having mastered the great classics, he said, the student pursued his calling without being disturbed by issues of depression and prosperity, war and peace, despotism and democracy, and the future of civilization.[3] Moreover, Counts attacked Hutchins's theory for ignoring the needed reconstruction of society.[4] In opposition to the argument that education consisted entirely of mental training through concentration on the classics, Counts stated that education was a process of inducting the young into the ways, privileges and responsibilities of a given society. To Counts, the study of a great living civilization ranked above that of the classics.[5]

Counts's criticisms of *The Higher Learning in America* merit special consideration since many opponents of a reconstructive philosophy of education derived their theories on such intellectual grounds. It is interesting to note further that both the theories of Hutchins and Counts, though widely varied, developed during the fertile period of ferment during the 1930s. For Counts, education was a function of a particular society at a given time and place. Culturally rooted, education expressed social needs and aspirations. In direct contrast to Counts and Dewey, Hutchins's theory rested on the assumption that essential and unchanging elements existed in human nature. Since he believed that human nature was everywhere the same, Hutchins stressed a universal system of education. As he stated in *The Higher Learning in America:*

> One purpose of education is to draw out the elements of our common human nature. These elements are the same in any time or place. The notion of educating man to live in any particular time or place, to adjust him to any particular environment, is therefore foreign to a true conception of education.
> Education implies teaching. Teaching implies knowledge. Knowledge is truth. The truth is everywhere the same. Hence education should be everywhere the same.[6]

The roots of the controversy between Hutchins and the Instrumentalism of Dewey, to which Counts adhered, concerned a basic epistemological difference. While Hutchins spoke of universal, absolute, and unchanging a priori truths and antecedent realities, the instrumentalists rejected predetermined ends and the existence of a priori, eternal verities.

Counts's attacks on pure intellectualism were oversimplified when he accused the products of intellectual education of refusing to enter into social controversies. Hutchins and many of his followers entered into the controversies of the day. Indeed, both Counts and Hutchins strove to reduce the widespread educational confusion. Both attacked the crass materialism which produced much of this confusion. Counts's attacks on purely intellectual education should not be conceived of as an anti-intellectual or an anti–subject matter approach. Counts believed that the experimental method had to be located within the existing conclusions of various subject fields which served as repositories of tested knowledge. However, these conclusions were not confined solely to great classics of Western civilization. For Counts, the inquiring and critical mind had to search beyond these classics into the latest and most definitive sociological, historical, psychological, and philosophical researches.

Although Hutchins's proposals spurred heated controversy in the 1930s, they have found continued support. Counts, in *Education and the Promise of America* (1946) and *Education and American Civilization* (1952), continued to attack the conception that education should serve solely intellectual purposes.

Education for Cultural Adjustment

Counts objected to the idea that in a dynamic society the major function of education should be that of preparing the individual for adjustment to society. He was referring to the traditional mode of education which prepared students to compete in the existent world rather than to attempt social reform. This kind of education drove man into competition with his neighbors and assumed him incapable of using the creations of his brain in the common interest. Counts charged the traditional form of education with adjustment-imposed chaos, cruelty, and ugliness [7] through acceptance of the status quo and indoctrination of the immature.

Counts stated that this traditional brand of education contained no great ideal capable of enlisting the loyalties and disciplining the energies of childhood and youth. In the light of economic individualism, children were nourished on moral platitudes bearing little or no relationship to social realities. The traditional educational philosophy rested upon the framework of economic individualism, which was divisive rather than unifying and tended to reduce society to the role of a policeman.[8] Although Counts was vague in attacking any definite traditional form of education, he probably referred to those educational policies which had patterned the American system of education in a competitive capitalistic society. Counts's entire educational program was specifically directed against an educational policy of drift which merely reflected the prevailing social scene.

Most likely, Counts was criticizing those claiming to be "essentialists" who attacked progressive educators for destroying the traditional disciplines of the curriculum, of attaching undue emphasis to the social studies, and of generally weakening the school program. Along with William C. Bagley, Counts's colleague I. L. Kandel at Teachers College criticized both progressive education and the attempts to use education for social reconstruction. To Kandel, it was incomprehensible

that the very same people who during the 1920s had advocated
individualism, freedom, the child-centered school, and the
sanctity of the child's personality were now often the very
same persons who called for social reconstruction through the
school with an emphasis on planning, cooperation, and collectivism.

The essentialists attacked both wings of progressive education: the advocates of the child-centered school and those of
the community-centered school. Their attacks were primarily
directed against the followers of Kilpatrick who urged the
project method, interests of the child, and a general deem-
phasis of subject matter during the early school years. In many
ways, Counts echoed their attacks on the overemphasis of the
child-centered school. Indeed, during the 1930s, Kilpatrick
had also joined the trend to the community-centered school
which Counts advocated. I. L. Kandel severely criticized the
progressive movement in education. Although not directly
attacking Counts, he argued against the notions of social reconstruction and imposition. Kandel charged that education
for a new social order closed the minds of pupils. He said that
for a society in transition, no one person or group had the final
answer. Kandel also stated that to instill ready-made ideas on
controversial issues or to influence pupils to accept one doctrine
rather than another was to confuse education with propaganda.
Finally, Kandel conceived of the role of the school as deriva-
tive from society rather than an originative force as did Counts.
Kandel stated that:

> There has, however, been injected into discussions of
> education and social change the suggestion that schools
> should, in a period of change, educate for a new social
> order, and that teachers, should ally themselves with

some political group and use their classrooms to propagate certain doctrines. Schools and teachers should, in other words, participate more directly and vitally in projecting particular ideas or patterns of social change and in their execution. The whole history of education emphasizes the impossibility of this idea, for society establishes schools to provide a firm basis for itself and to sustain the common interest. Schools are a part of the environment which they serve; they are not autonomous or insulated against the social forces and influences around them; nor can teachers on the basis of a guess as to the active forces of the day help to build a new social order. Society changes first and schools follow.[9]

Kandel and Counts were not in complete disagreement, however. Both educators believed that the schools were part of society and served to introduce the immature to society. To Kandel, this introduction occurred through the mediation of the traditional essential curriculum of language, number, science, and history. For Counts, this curriculum, too, fulfilled part of the residual function of the school. Although he relied on a subject matter approach as did the essentialists, Counts did not rely solely on the mediating influence of the essential subjects. For him, the curriculum had to adjust to social change since values had to be repatterned as society changed. Following Dewey, Counts accepted the function of the school as a purifying agency; the essentialists seemed rather to regard the forces in society as a selecting agency. Once this had been done by society, then the school would follow the social dictation. For Counts, the dominant forces in society selected the value pattern inculcated in the schools. Since the dominant forces controlled society and, thus, the school, unless the educational profession intervened, the values taught by the school would reflect the undemocratic tendencies prized by the dominant social groups. This seemed to be a major point of controversy between the reconstructionist, Counts, and the traditionalist or essentialist, Kandel.

The Scientific Movement in Education

Counts received his early training at the University of Chicago under Charles Judd, a leader in the scientific movement in American education. His doctoral dissertation "Arithmetic Tests and Studies in the Psychology of Arithmetic" (1917) reflected the emphasis of the scientific movement. _The Selective Character of American Education_ (1922), _The Senior High School Curriculum_ (1926), and _The Social Composition of Boards of Education_ (1927) used statistical analysis but reached broader social conclusions. By the time of the publication of _School and Society in Chicago_ (1928) and _Secondary Education and Industrialism_ (1929) Counts was well on the way to emphasizing the sociological implications of education which characterized his work since the 1930s. Reflecting his training in sociology under Albion W. Small and W. I. Thomas, Counts embarked on a socio-historical study of the problems of education.[10] In the 1930s Counts questioned some of the influences of the scientific movement upon education.

In _The American Road to Culture_ (1930) Counts appraised the scientific movement as being too preoccupied with the machinery and externals of education.[11] In _The Social Foundations of Education_ (1934) he further attacked the excesses of efforts to create a science of education. Since the turn of the century, he said, unflagging efforts attempted reduction of educational problems to simple formulae. Quantitative methods were applied to learning processes, methods of teaching, and aspects of school administration. School systems were surveyed; objective tests, scales, and scorecards standardized for measurements of intelligence, school attainment, teaching ability, administrative efficiency, and almost every other phase of the educational conduct. All of these areas were measured and evaluated quantitatively in the hope of reducing all educational problems to rapid and impersonal solutions.[12]

Although energy was expended and data accumulated, Counts feared that much of this labor was irrelevant or trivial. The emphasis of building a science of education focused the educators' attention on the application of quantitative procedures to the simple, mechanical, and less significant aspects of education. Instead of investigating the meaning for education of the shift from the individualistic agrarian economy to urbanized society, educators engaged in fashioning spelling scales or score cards. With this immersion in searching for a science of education, Counts found that the education profession had really sought to escape the pressing problems of cultural transition and economic dislocation.[13]

Further, Counts said the search for a science of education ignored the axiological criteria present at the core of all educational problems. Matters involving the selection or rejection of values were barred from consideration on the grounds that they were subjective and outside the purvue of educational science. This narrow pedagogical approach placed the scientific movement in education on the side of the dominant forces interested in perpetuation of the status quo. In their preoccupation with measurement, the scientific inquirers accepted the traditional framework of institutions, ideas, and values. The impact of the depression of the 1930s on public education had not been anticipated by those immersed in the scientific study of education. Counts found that the foundations of the educational system and society which they had measured so carefully were already in a process of disintegration.[14]

In addition to ignoring the cultural framework of education, Counts charged that the exaltation of the scientific movement in education favored the mere elaboration of educational techniques and elevated the role of the administrator to the detriment of the classroom teacher. If education was conceived of solely as tests, scales, and classifications, then persons located at the administrative center of the school could guide the program. Counts stated:

> One need not even know the content of a particular subject which he is supervising, if he has at hand objective tests which, when administered according to carefully outlined directions reveal as unerringly as a thermometer in its field the precise condition of the learner. If the tests are supplemented by a knowledge of method, the supervisor can pass judgment not only on the product, but also on the process of instruction.[15]

Counts believed that the pressing problems of economic disorganization and profound cultural transition had finally turned American educators away from trivialities and mechanics to fundamental inquiry regarding the social purpose of the school. In a proposal to enlarge the scope of the historical and cultural foundations of education at Columbia University, Counts wrote that educational literature was not sufficiently concerned with the problems of goals, objectives, and purposes. Since the complete absorption in methods, mechanics, and physical aspects of education was passing, he felt social crisis had forced organized education to reconsider controlling principles and philosophy.[16] A later chapter on teacher education will deal more fully with the aspects of methodology and the effects of the scientific movement on teacher preparation. It is sufficient at this time to conclude that Counts was severely disillusioned with the program of the scientific movement in organized education.

Counts did not confine his criticisms of the scientific movement in education solely to the depression period when social implications were highly emphasized. In his lectures to Brazilian educators in 1962, Counts's criticisms of the scientific movement in education were similar to those of the 1930s. Once again he accused the scientific movement of taking the traditional program of the school for granted and placing emphasis on mere increased mechanical efficiency. This emphasis, he warned, reduced education to an autonomous process isolated from society and civilization and perfected according to its own laws. Although the scientific movement contributed much of value to education, a more generous conception of a science of education was needed. In urging a science that was closely integrated with society and culture, he admonished: "Science can penetrate the secrets of the atom, but it cannot tell us whether we should make atomic bombs convert atomic energy to peaceful purposes. Such questions lie in the realm of ethics and politics." [17]

Lest confusion arise, it must be stated that Counts advocated the free inquiry of the instrumentalist philosophy based upon the scientific method. When he attacked the scientific movement in education, he was not attacking the scientific method; rather he was criticizing the subordination of the scientific method to a mere study of learning processes by quantitative means. He urged educational researchers to do more than merely measure and count. The data compiled by educational researchers had to be harmonized with some theory of the good, just, and beautiful and had to be related definitely to some order of society. The scientific movement in education had ignored this formidable challenge.

The Progressive Movement in Education

The major part of this treatment of Counts's analysis of the responses of education during the 1930s will be devoted to the progressive movement in education. In February of 1932, Counts addressed the twelfth annual meeting of the Progressive Education Association at Baltimore, Maryland. His address "Dare Progressive Education be Progressive?" was a virtual bombshell. Counts censured progressive education for lacking a social program, ignoring the problems of cultural transition and economic depression, and continuing to rely on the child-centered school. He also lauded the many achievements of progressive education which had focused attention on the child. Although these achievements significantly contributed to educational theory and practice, they were inadequate responses to the pressing needs of contemporary society. Counts urged progressive education to liberate itself from domination by the upper middle class, to face the current social problems, to fashion a realistic and comprehensive theory of social welfare, and to come to grips with the problems of cultural transition and economic depression. Counts called upon progressive educators to define their purposes clearly so that the movement which they represented would be genuinely forward moving.[18]

The Progressive Education Journal reported that Counts's

address had provoked vigorous discussion. Counts had affirmed that the school should chart a program of social reconstruction. Although it was generally agreed that the school had such responsibility, the journal recorded considerable differences among Progressives on how to implement this task. The journal added that there was widespread fear of the indoctrination that Counts seemed to imply.[19] Needless to say, Counts's message stirred controversy in the association; later in the same year, Counts enlarged his audience and issued much the same message in his famous *Dare the School Build a New Social Order?* The words in the messages of 1932 revealed the hopes, fears, and disappointments of the depression-ridden generation of American educators. Merle Curti in *The Social Ideas of American Educators,* 1935, marked this address as a turning point in American education; Adolph Meyer in *The Development of Education in the Twentieth Century,* 1939, pointed to the ferment unleashed by Counts's arguments; and Lawrence Cremin in *The Transformation of the School: Progressivism in American Education,* 1962, continued to attach importance to Counts's address.[20] In the light of the attention focused upon his *Dare the School Build a New Social Order?* by these and other interpreters of American education, some attention should be paid to Counts's efforts of 1932.

Before entering into his criticism of progressive education, Counts surveyed the achievements which it made to educational theory and practice in the United States. Of all the educational groups, Counts believed the progressive education movement demonstrated the greatest promise of genuine and creative leadership through two great American faiths: faith in progress and faith in education. From this union, Counts stated that hope remained for light and guidance.

Progressive education had a large number of achievements to its credit. It had broken with the traditional modes of education by focusing attention on the child. It had successfully defended the thesis that activity rested at the root of all true education. Under its guidance, learning was conceived in terms of life situations and the growth of character. It had championed the rights of the child as a unique personality. Counts was proud of these achievements by a movement in which he shared both interest and effort. Although progressive educators had made excellent contributions to American education in the past, the exclusive focus on the nature of the child was insufficient to cope with the crisis of cultural transition and economic depression. Counts asserted that this was "too narrow a conception of the meaning of education." [21]

Weakness of Progressive Education

Counts attributed the weaknesses of the progressive education movement to its failure to elaborate a theory of social welfare. More specifically, this general weakness was due to four factors: trust in the child-centered school; a middle-class orientation; the conception of the school as an all-powerful educational agency; and a false notion of freedom.

As already stated, progressivism had liberated the child from rote and drill educational methods. Many of the recommendations of the scientific movement have been readily adopted by the more progressive schools. Private progressive schools had implemented the findings of child study. In their sole concern for child welfare and growth, progressives failed to elaborate an adequate theory of social welfare to guide their educational activity. As a result, progressive educators substituted the child-centered school for positive thought and action. Counts concluded that progressive education could no longer base its program solely on the foundations of the child-centered school.[22]

Counts contended that there was a large degree of middle-class bias and control in the program and support of progressive education. Progressive education reflected the viewpoint of the liberal-minded upper-middle class who sent their children to the private progressive schools. Counts stated that these middle-class patrons of progressive schools were financially well off and assumed an indifferent attitude toward all important social questions. In defense of their social cynicism, they prided themselves on open-mindedness and tolerance. Although they possessed vague aspirations for world peace and human brotherhood, Counts stated that they possessed no deep and abiding loyalties and were often insensitive to accepted forms of social injustice.[23]

Among the middle class, Counts continued, the number of children was low and the amount of income relatively high. Freed from pressing financial concerns, an inordinate emphasis was placed on the child and his interests. Wishing to protect their offspring from strenuous effort and an intimate contact with industrial society, they isolated their children from the realities of life in modern society. Motivated by class standards and achievements, these middle-class patrons of progressive schools felt themselves superior and did not want their children contaminated by too many contacts with the children of the poor or the less favored races.[24] In times of trial, he concluded, the middle class followed the lead of the most respected and powerful forces in society. Counts indicted the middle class as a group of "romantic sentimentalists" who had clearly demonstrated their incapacity to deal with the great crises of "war, prosperity, or depression." It was unlikely that the middle class could be relied upon to direct the course of American education.[25]

Counts urged that if progressive education was to be genuinely progressive, it had to emancipate itself from the influence of the middle class and squarely face the pressing social problems besetting contemporary society. In developing an intimate relationship with the community, it had to fashion a realistic and comprehensive theory of welfare and cast off fear of the bogies of imposition and indoctrination. Progressive education could not continue to rely solely on the child-centered school dominated by middle-class attitudes.

In his criticism of the middle class, Counts revealed a definite prejudice on behalf of the lower economic groups of farmers and laborers. Many times in his writings during the 1930s, he urged the teaching profession to ally itself in the class struggle with the laboring masses. In his social analysis, he condemned the tendency on the part of an "economic aristocracy" to dominate American society. Especially in *The Prospects of American Democracy,* he condemned this minority which presided at the summit of the economic hierarchy.

In viewing the origins of much of political and economic reformism in American history, the middle classes had contributed greatly to the rise of such reform movements as the progressive movement of the first two decades of the twentieth century. This very group that Counts condemned had supported Robert La Follette, Theodore Roosevelt, and Woodrow Wilson in their efforts to restrict the growth of economic monopolies and trusts and to curb the growth of plutocracy in the United States. In its origins much of the progressive movement in education reflected the growth of political progressivism. Many of those who urged educational reforms were of middle-class backgrounds. Counts may have been too severe in his criticisms of the middle class as social reformers.

A certain degree of truth undoubtedly surrounded his charge that the middle class isolated their children from the realities of the industrial age. In his analysis of American education in *The American Road to Culture* (1930) Counts pointed to the tendency of Americans to view education as a means of improving social and economic status and thus achieving individualized social betterment. The middle class was not the only group to conceive of the benefits of education in this light. The lower economic groups also went to the door of the school as a means of entrance into an improved social and economic position.

Finally, it might be stated that the middle class may have feared such a sweeping program as that advocated by Counts. With vested economic interests such as small shops, businesses, and enterprises, they may well have feared the consequences of a sweeping program of economic collectivism. Although Counts feared that the encroachments of the "economic aristocracy" would render such small enterprises obsolete as larger and larger economic consolidations occurred, the small middle-class businessman may have feared for the survival of his economic independence.

Next, Counts turned his attack on what he called the fallacy that the school was an all-powerful educational agency. For Counts, the school was only one of many educational agencies. Like most professional groups, the leaders of the progressive education movement exaggerated their own importance and stressed the idea that the school was an all-powerful educational agency. Counts said Progressives constantly talked about reconstructing society through education; and on the other hand, they lived in perpetual fear that the school would impose some point of view upon all children and mold them into a single pattern. Counts said that life was too complex in modern society to permit this; the school was but one of many formative agencies. The school could not remain aloof from the other educational agencies such as the home, church, labor union, press, motion picture, or political party. Counts stated that progressive educators should use whatever power they possessed in opposing and checking the forces of social reaction. To be effective, he concluded, the school needed the support of other agencies.[26] Counts urged progressive educators to abandon attempts to isolate the school from the mainspring of the social, political, and economic conflicts existent in contemporary society.

Counts concluded his criticism with a discussion of the Progressive misconceptions of freedom. By failing to develop a satisfactory social orientation, Progressives were victims of a misleading conception of the nature of human freedom and an inadequate view of the positive role of adults in the education of the immature. Due to the stress placed on the freedom and interests of the child, many Progressives opposed any attempt at imposition. Counts believed that such a sweeping denunciation of all adult imposition as a form of authoritarian indoctrination put teachers in an untenable position. For without some degree of imposition, it was impossible to educate.[27] Although some Progressives agreed that some degree of imposition was necessary to educate, Counts stated that they refused to understand, plan, or control the process. Although progressive education wished to build a new world, Counts stated that it refused to be held accountable for the kind of world it built. In speaking of the progressives' refusal to commit themselves to ordering the process of educational imposition, Counts stated: "They will admit that the child is molded by his environment, and then presumably contend that in the fashioning of this environment we should close our eyes to the consequences of our acts in the light of definite knowledge of their consequences." [28] Because he urged educational imposition, Counts encountered the opposition of Progressives who advocated educational neutrality. In the chapter on "Imposition," this problem has been treated in more detail. Counts made educational history at the Progressive Education Association meeting of 1932 when he took the association to task for its refusal to deal with pressing social problems.

The meeting was torn by the ferment released by Counts's comments. As arguments ranged pro and con, a mood for deliberate action swept the association. Counts succeeded in diverting the attention of progressive educators from concentration on the child-centered school to a consideration of the great problems inherent in building a new social order.

A Call to the Teachers of the Nation

On February 20, 1932, Nellie Seeds, director of the Manumit School of Pawling, New York, sponsored a resolution which urged the Progressive Education Association to accept Counts's challenge "to build a new social order." The Seeds resolution called for the appointment of an economics and sociology section or committee within the Progressive Education Association to "promote within the schools and their affiliated bodies, thoughtful and systematic study of the economic and industrial problems confronting the world today." [29]

After the passage of the Seeds resolution, the board of directors of the Progressive Education Association appointed at their meeting at Vassar College in April of 1932, the Committee on Social and Economic Problems with George Counts as chairman. Included among the members of the committee were such scholars as Merle E. Curti, Sidney Hook, Jesse Newlon, Willard Beatty, John Gambs, Charles Easton, Goodwin Watson, and Frederick Redefer. In commissioning the committee to investigate the pressing social and economic problems, the directors of the Progressive Education Association expressed general agreement that the school of the future had to be much more than child centered and that the development of individuality did not necessarily insure the development of social consciousness. An adequate school program required an adequate social program. The schools' problem in the critical age of the depression was to study the nature of the conflicts present in society and to develop the moral and intellectual fiber necessary to cope with the age of great social change.[30]

In March of 1933, the Committee on Social and Economic Problems, headed by Counts reported to the board of directors of the Progressive Education Association. This report, published in 1933 as *A Call to the Teachers of the Nation,* urged recognition of the corporate and interdependent character of the contemporary social order and recommended the transference of the democratic traditions from individualistic to collectivistic economic foundations. The report urged the abandonment of the doctrines of laissez faire and, like Counts's *Dare the School Build a New Social Order?,* pleaded for bold social experimentation. Much of the content of this report has already been discussed in relation to Counts's analysis of socioeconomic questions.

Upon hearing the report, the board of directors of the Progressive Education Association lost some of their enthusiasm for social reconstruction. According to Cremin, Carleton

Washburne questioned the advisability of giving any committee report the right to speak on behalf of the association. He further advised that educators were already under too much pressure and should not invite further antagonism by committing the schools to a new social utopia.[31] The pamphlet containing the report of the Counts committee was published independently of the association and contained an introduction by President Willard Beatty which stated: "The publication of a report of such a Committee does not commit either the Board of Directors of the Association or the members of the Association, individually or as a whole, to any program or policy embodied in the report." [32]

Despite the initial enthusiasm for Counts's address as demonstrated by Miss Seeds and other progressives, the bloom soon faded as is illustrated by President Beatty's noncommittal introduction to the report of the committee which was created by the association. The lack of commitment on the part of the Progressive Education Association indicated that it, for the most part, still was suspicious of imposition and attempts to interfere with the existing social order in any direct way. Nevertheless, the report of the committee and Counts's address established a relation between the association and social reformism from which it never escaped.

Although, as already mentioned, the message of *A Call to the Teachers of the Nation* has been examined in the analysis of Counts's social theory, the Committee recommended a selected bibliography to the teachers of the nation. A brief look at this bibliography suggests somewhat the orientation of the participants on the committee and of Counts himself. The committee recommended Charles and Mary Beard's *The Rise of American Civilization* (1930) not only as excellent history from the general point of view, but also as excellent economic history.[33] Counts and Beard were associates on the Commission of the American Historical Association on the Social Studies in the Schools during the early 1930s. In addition to their professional collaboration, they were also very close personal friends.[34] Childs says that Counts's interest in the relation of organized education to American public affairs was deepened and enriched through his association with the Beards.[35] In *Education and American Civilization* (1952) Counts acknowledged his debt to the works of John Dewey and Charles A. Beard. In these works, he said, there stemmed a vigorous movement for educational reform and reconstruction which increasingly gave attention to the role of community and culture in the educational process and the importance of relating school and all educational agencies to social life.[36]

Reflecting the attention devoted to economic forces during the depression period, the committee recommended Berle and Means, *The Modern Corporation and Private Property* (1932). This work which Counts had cited as an important source in his social analysis in *The Prospects of American Democracy* (1938) discussed the concentration of economic power in the United States. The committee rated it as extremely important among recent books on economics and suited for required reading by all teachers.[37] Another book on the contemporary depression climate of opinion was recommended: Louis Adamic, *Dynamite* (1931). In its recommendation, the committee stated that it was a story of class violence in the United States by an author who was sympathetic to labor. It had additional value as a partial history of the American labor movement and as an analysis of the present disintegration of that movement.[38]

Of special interest was the inclusion of two works published during the period of Populist discontent, Edward Bel-

lamy's *Looking Backward* (1888) and Henry George's
Progress and Poverty (1879). These two books introduced the
American reading public to the alleged benefits of a planned
social order. The committee characterized *Looking Backward*
as "a lively romance which, in the eighties, stirred the entire
nation." They quoted the Beards who termed it, "the first
utopia of applied science—which naturalized socialism and
baptized it in the name of business efficiency." [39] *Progress and
Poverty* was found to be a strictly American classic of economic
protest which drew the deadly parallel of riches and misery.[40]

The inclusion of George and Bellamy in the reading list
of the nation's teachers revealed a return to the origins of
American democratic collectivism. Much of Counts's work resembled a modernized version of the protests of the muck-
rakers, the program of the Populists, and the reforms of the
pre–World War I Progressives. Although he drew attention
to the impact of science and technology, he also protested
strongly against social, political, and economic inequality. Unlike the protests of European scientific socialism, Counts never
despaired of the efficacy of the American political processes.
In much the same way, his educational program and philosophy mainly rested on an interpretation of the works of Dewey.

The Social Frontier

Since the Progressive Education Association failed to commit itself to a deliberate program of social inquiry and reconstruction, Counts and other proponents of a new social order
looked elsewhere. A journal of social reformist attitudes, *Social Frontier,* was launched in 1934 under the chairmanship
of William H. Kilpatrick and under the editorial guidance of

George S. Counts. The editor of the new journal clearly indicated the social reconstructionist orientation of *Social Frontier*, which was to be a vehicle for uniting and articulating the ideas of those persons who wanted to move American society and education toward the emergent social order. Counts's initial editorial asserted that the journal was conceived as a means of expressing the commonly shared commitments and aspirations of persons who had hitherto worked in isolation:

> Before these persons, and perhaps countless others who have thus far remained inarticulate, can hope to become a positive creative force in American society and education, they must come into closer communication, clarify their thought and purposes, draw like-minded individuals into their ranks, and merge isolated and discordant voices into a mighty instrument of group consensus, harmonious expression, and collective action.[41]

The editors of *Social Frontier* pretended no absolute objectivity and detachment. Reflecting a definite point of view, its frame of reference rested on a particular interpretation of American history. First, the journal determined to fight for preservation of the ideals of freedom of speech, cultural diversity, personal liberty, security, and dignity. Secondly, it regarded economic goods not as the chief end of life, but as a basis and means of enriching cultural development; the only hope for the freedom of the majority rested in the establishing of democratic control over the material sources of life. The complicated mechanism of modern industrial society demanded coordination, unified direction, and control. Third, education had an important part in the clarification of issues and alignment of forces. Education, school, and teacher had to play a role commensurate with the power of the institutions and persons involved. No educational journal could remain neutral on important questions of this kind. Fourth, *Social Frontier* strove for a form of collectivism that made paramount the interests of the overwhelming majority of the population. Accepting the rise of a collectivistic order as an inevitable consequence of industrialization, the journal maintained that American collectivism could be democratic.[42]

Social Frontier was not confined solely to the work of the school as were other educational journals. While recognizing the school as society's central educational agency, it went beyond mere consideration of the activities of the school. It surveyed all those formative influences and agencies which inducted the individual into cultural life. It regarded education as an aspect of a culture in the process of evolution.[43] A socially construed education determined the content and form of society since society changed because of the dynamic elements within it. Education was one of these dynamic elements.[44]

With this Countian declaration of purposes, the career of *Social Frontier* was launched. During the decade of its life, the articles in *Social Frontier* ranged from examinations of collectivism to support for teacher organization. Among the members of its board of directors were many notables in the field of social and educational inquiry, such as W. H. Kilpatrick, John Childs, John Dewey, Sidney Hook, H. Gordon Hullfish, Jesse Newlon, Harry A. Overstreet, R. Bruce Raup, Harold Rugg, V. T. Thayer, and Goodwin Watson.

The *Social Frontier* gained considerable attention during the depression period when its leaders were denounced by the Hearst Press and the National Association of Manufacturers as Marxists and Reds.[45] Curti said that Marxism was only one and not the most important factor in the social thinking of this group: "The antithesis between almost everything that the Soviet Union stood for and the democratic values to which the Social Frontier group was dedicated, was increasingly clear." [46] The concluding part of this paper will consider Counts's theory in relation to theoretical Marxism. Despite Curti's disavowal of Marxism on the part of *Social Frontier*, William R. Hearst thought differently.

Hearst ordered that Counts's name was not to be mentioned in any of his publications. An article in *Time* entitled "Unmentionable Counts" discussed the ban on Counts and commented that Hearst exaggerated Counts's radicalism. It stated that Counts's message was broad in idea and general in language and failed to reduce the theme of economic democracy to concrete proposals. The article concluded that Counts's use of the word "collectivist," his two trips to Russia, and his criticisms of the American Legion, Hearst newspapers, teachers' loyalty oaths, and the Liberty League really did more to build up the reputation of radicalism than all the New Dealish effusions contained in his pleas for an "economic democracy." [47]

Some aspects of the influence of *Social Frontier* might be clarified by briefly examining some editorial comments which appeared in leading newspapers concerning the launching of the journal. The *New York Times* commented that the appearance of the journal was newsworthy not only because of its alleged freedom, but also because of its personnel. The editor and directors were nearly all men who were born, reared, and educated in areas that were some distance from the great urban centers of population. Coming from Kansas, Nebraska, Indiana, Georgia, and Vermont, they were descended from the old American stock. The *New York Times* concluded: "That men of such high professional knowledge and strong patriotic purpose should undertake this venture will at any rate lead to fresh appraisement of educational values in the face of the changing order and make against the lethargy into which fixed systems are so apt to lead." [48]

This brief comment in the *New York Times* called attention to a significant detail concerning Counts and many like-minded educational theorists. They were men who were still close to the American frontier tradition. Counts was born in rural Kansas and his ideas were permeated by the spirit of frontier egalitarianism. His interpretation of democracy and industrial society, although framed in technological phraseology, still hearkened back to these frontier origins.

The *Indianapolis News* did not reflect the generous attitude of the *New York Times* in its editorial comments. The *News* found the announcement of the birth of *Social Frontier* to be a vague indication of Russian Sovietism. It stated that the editors definitely opposed the right of the individual to strive for self-improvement and wished all persons reduced to the same level of mediocrity. The *News* commented "it would be interesting to know whether the editor of the new publication and his associates have been taking advantage of the profit system since they were old enough to shift for themselves." [49]

The Bridgeport *Telegram* levied the charge of Communist influence against the fledging journal. This charge was often repeated during the life of *Social Frontier*. The *Telegram* stated "Russia today is the prime example of the society for which Dr. Counts and his fellow workers, Dr. William H. Kilpatrick and Professor Dewey are striving. It has abolished the profit system and its "special motivation is a collective classlessness," to paraphrase the academic phraseology of Dr. Counts." [50]

On the basis of these brief newspaper comments, a common charge levied against Counts was that of advocating communism for the United States. Before turning to a consideration of this charge, it would be appropriate to conclude the discussion of *Social Frontier*. Throughout this book, comments and evidence have been used from *Social Frontier* to explicate Counts's position during the 1930s. The comments which launched *Social Frontier* revealed the same general orientation which Counts shared. Counts continued to edit the journal until 1937. George Hartmann of Teachers College, Columbia University, edited the journal from 1937 until 1939. The Progressive Education Association took over the journal and changed its name to *Frontiers of Democracy* in 1939. It was edited from 1939 until 1943 by William H. Kilpatrick and James L. Hymes. The magazine died in 1943 after the remaining few issues were edited by Harold Rugg.

Communist Influences

Since the question of communist influences on Counts was raised during the 1930s, this section on educational responses during the depression period would be incomplete without some consideration of this question. At the outset of this discussion, however, certain qualifications should be made. First, a complete analysis of Counts's relations and attitudes to the Soviet Union can be made only through an exhaustive study of his Russian works. Second, Counts's attitudes toward Soviet communism during the 1930s are not precisely the same thing as his relationships to theoretical Marxism. Although Russian communism cannot be understood without a knowledge of Marxism, it is possible to enter into a discussion of theoretical Marxism without a detailed discussion of Russian communism.

The author wishes to reserve the discussion of Counts's relationships with theoretical Marxism until the concluding section of this work. With these two qualifications stated, a
discussion of the allegation of communist influence on the
thought of Counts follows.

In 1927, Counts and other American academicians accompanied the technical staff of the first American trade union
delegation to the Soviet Union. Upon his return, Counts wrote
of his Russian experience and prepared reports on the Soviet
educational system. He was generally impressed with the vigor
and magnitude of Soviet education and the creative role assigned to the schools. Upon his return to Teachers College
and as associate director of its International Institute, Counts
became this country's foremost student of the Soviet educational system.[51] Impressed with the Soviet achievements in industrial planning, Counts wrote in *The Soviet Challenge to
America* (1931) that: "Ideas are among the most dynamic elements in human culture; and the Russian revolution has released ideas, as have very few of the social convulsions of history." [52]

Counts began his appraisal of the effects of the first Soviet
Five Year Plan, 1928–33, on the Russian educational system
with a discussion of dialectical materialism, collectivism, equality of nationalities, equality of the sexes, the Soviet Army,
Communist party, and Russian government. This discussion
was objective and primarily descriptive rather than analytical
and *The Soviet Challenge to America* read much like a text
book of Russian history since the Bolshevik Revolution. Although, at this time, Counts stressed the importance of the
Soviet Communist party, he attributed almost equal significance to these other areas of Soviet life. He seemed to have

fallen victim to stating the letter of the Soviet constitution rather than deeply penetrating the underlying political realities.

In 1931, Counts was more concerned with social planning in the Soviet Union than in the politics of the Russian Communist party. He stated that the principle of social planning distinguished education in the Soviet Union from that in the United States. Social planning left its imprint upon the purpose, organization, support, and curriculum of Russian education. In the Soviet Union, planning raised basic questions concerning the position of the teacher, the question of indoctrination, the nature of freedom, and the integration of culture. Counts concluded that these important educational tasks had been ignored in the United States.[53]

Counts was greatly impressed by the stress on activity in the Soviet schools. Although American education was remote from life experience, Soviet education emphasized activities with a definite purpose in mind. With a strong collectivist bias, activity was devoted to promotion of community welfare. Activity in the Soviet schools was to a very large degree socially useful labor. This was in striking contrast to the activity of the American progressive schools which stressed activity for the sake of activity.[54] Counts was equally impressed with the Soviet use of all educative media for the promotion of collectivization. Radio, school, youth organizations, press, party, lectures, and museums promoted either an information or propaganda offensive for the Five Year Plan which gave youth a mission to perform. Once again Soviet education presented sharp contrast to the purposelessness of American education which at times even feared to impose democracy upon its charges.

Counts was not inspired by Marxian dogma or by the machinery of the Communist party of the Soviet Union. Rather he was impressed by the process of making a backward agricultural nation into a powerful industrialized giant. He was equally impressed by the importance which the Soviet Union attached to its education system and to its young people in the program for leaping into the modern world.

Counts demonstrated a certain amount of naïveté in his brief discussion of political life in the Soviet Union which appeared in *The Soviet Challenge to America*. During the very years that Stalin was consolidating personal authority in the Soviet Union, Counts wrote that while there was a dictatorship in the Soviet Union, it was not a personal dictatorship of any one man or even any small group of men. The Communist party apparatus, he said, was not a mere mechanism in the hands of an autocrat but was rather an organism throbbing with life in every one of its thousands of separate cells. Through discussion in these cells, gradually the party would survive any individual. The party line was the product of the collective mind and could alter its course at any time. So powerful was this collective mind that even Stalin had to yield to its will.[55] Counts was naïve in his early reviews of the Stalin dictatorship which in the early 1930s was beginning the purging of party deviationists such as the Trotskyites and the elimination of the small peasant land holders, the *kulaks,* and the small businessmen, representatives of the New Economic Policy.

Counts was confused on the idea of self-criticism in the Soviet Union. Although today, the elaborate self-criticisms and confessions of the purged functionaries are known to have been carefully planned and rehearsed, Counts saw them as genuine expressions of remorse on the part of officials and workers. Once again as he had relied on the written Soviet Constitution for his ideas concerning the operations of the

Russian government, he relied on press statements from the purged party functionaries. Counts translated statements of the Soviet Press regarding the self-criticisms of the left deviationists, Zinoviev and Kamenev, and of the right deviationists, Tomsky, Bukharin, and Rykov, who were purged by the Stalinist machinery. Counts compared the self-critical statements of these old Bolsheviks to the lack of such statements by Western politicians. He said that these statements of self-criticism revealed the operation of powerful psychological forces which were without counterpart in the West.[56] Counts misunderstood the nature of self-criticism which really signified the coming purges of the Stalinist period.

Despite Counts's early naïveté regarding the operational practices of the Soviet Communist party, he showed a surprising amount of foresight. At a time when many Western observers waited daily for the collapse of the Soviet Union, Counts warned of the Soviet challenge to the West:

> While generations will have to come and go before that experiment can be accurately appraised in all of its departments, quite possibly the stage is being set for one of the most stupendous acts of history—the open and conscious competition between two radically different social systems. Christendom may be facing its most severe test since the disciples of Islam carried the crescent through the outer gates of Europe. That this competition may be peaceful should be the devout wish of all who feel any concern whatsoever regarding the future of mankind.[57]

Thus from these brief observations, a glimpse of Counts's reactions to the Soviet experiment of the 1930s can be gained.

Counts was not overly concerned with the role of the Communist party. He was impressed with the Soviet attempts to create an industrial society through the Five Year Plans. Counts was more impressed with Soviet modernization than with communist ideology. Unfortunately some of his critics in the United States branded Counts as a communist sympathizer because of his interests in the Soviet Union and its educational system.

By 1938, Counts's *The Prospects of American Democracy* warned those wishing to emulate the Soviet experiment that any attempt to extend democracy in the United States to the economic realm could not imitate the Russian pattern. Counts altered his first impressions of the Soviet Union. In the name of democracy, he charged a dictatorship of the proletariat had been set up. In actual practice, this was really a dictatorship of the party. The party, in turn, was controlled by a handful of men who claimed to represent the party and the proletariat but, in reality, served their own power lust. Thus, the Russian experience was unsuited for American imitation. He concluded that Russian communism repudiated free political institutions and inaugurated a regime of minority rule and strict censorship of speech and thought.[58] In *The Schools Can Teach Democracy* (1939) Counts further warned that the Russian revolution had been corrupted by the exigencies of personal ambition, ruthless dictatorship, cultural backwardness, and world tensions and conflicts.[59] Thus, at the very time when many liberal scholars were condoning popular front movements with the Communists, Counts condemned any such alliance.

Counts did not confine his anticommunism to foreign affairs. He also attacked the communist infiltration of the American teaching profession. During the depression period, teachers began to organize in larger numbers in the American Federation of Teachers which was affiliated with the American Federation of Labor. The college teachers of New York City organized Local 537 of this union. In the 1939 elections for officers of this local, Counts led a slate which unsuccessfully attempted to wrest control away from the communist sympathizers which controlled the local. It was decided to carry the fight against the Communists and their sympathizers to the national convention of the American Federation of Teachers. Almost immediately following the conclusion of the Molotov-Ribentrop Pact of 1939, the Convention of the American Federation of Teachers elected Counts as president in a close election in which he defeated the incumbent Davis by only twenty-four votes.[60] After his election, Counts led the union until 1942 during which time he continually fought communist infiltration. In 1943, with John L. Childs, he published *America, Russia, and the Communist Party in the Postwar World.* This official pronouncement of the American Federation of Teachers labeled the American Communist party as a liability to mutual understanding and collaboration between the Soviet Union and the United States. It termed the American Communist party an arm of the Communist International, controlled by Moscow, and committed to world revolution. As a disciplined, conspiratorial group, it was distinctly alien to American society.[61] Counts's devotion to the democratic ethic was so strong that only the most uncritical observers could genuinely label him as a communist sympathizer.

Counts remains an unrelenting critic of Soviet aims and educational practices. In his translation of the Soviet education textbook *I Want to Be Like Stalin* (1947) Counts stated that organized education in the Soviet Union was the handmaiden of politics. Education was a weapon for strengthening the Soviet state; the school was regarded as a powerful and indispensable organ of the Communist party, government, economy, army, and political police.[62] Counts warned in this volume, written shortly after the close of World War II, of the possibility of future armed conflict. The Russians, he said, were undoubtedly preparing for war. To avoid the conflict, the people of the free world had to move swiftly toward the establishment of an international police force. The establishment of free communication between the peoples of the Soviet Union and the United States was necessary to achieve peace. If the Russians refused to cooperate, the United States was compelled to prepare for the day of eventual conflict.[63]

In *Education and American Civilization* (1952) Counts again departed from his analysis of American society to warn the American people regarding the menace of Soviet communism to free societies. He stated that the Communist party was organized like an army under the high command in Moscow. It ruled the Soviet peoples and directed the struggle to vanquish the free nations of the world. Russian communism was a reactionary force engaged in an imperialistic drive. Wherever it went, it destroyed the last vestige of individual freedom and subjected men to tyranny.[64]

In summation, it can be stated that Counts found many of the educational responses of the 1930s inadequate to the challenges of cultural transition and economic depression. He rejected the notions of education as being solely intellectual, or based on an essential curriculum, or the product of educational science. Although the Progressive education movement contained the spark of needed educational reforms, it was confused as to direction and was too slow to move to respond to the crucial issues of the day. Totalitarian communism offered neither an educational nor political program acceptable to genuine democrats. After appraising the milieu of educational theory during the 1930s, Counts turned to his own approach to education which was based on a social philosophy of democratic collectivism. It is on Counts's own particular educational response that the following chapter focuses.

1. Counts, *The Social Foundations of Education* (New York: Charles Scribner's Sons, 1934), p. 536.

2. Counts, *Dare the Schools Build a New Social Order?* (New York: John Day Co., 1932), p. 21.

3. Counts, *Education and the Promise of America* (New York: Macmillan Co., 1946), pp. 23–24.

4. "Educating for Tomorrow," *Social Frontier*, 1 (1934), 6.

5. Counts, *Education and American Civilization* (New York: Bureau of Publications, Teachers College, Columbia University, 1953), p. 33.

6. Robert M. Hutchins, *The Higher Learning in America* (New Haven: Yale University Press, 1936), p. 66.

7. Counts, *Dare the Schools*, p. 27.

8. Counts, *Social Foundations*, p. 543.

9. I. L. Kandel, *Conflicting Theories of Education* (New York: Macmillan Co., 1938), p. 86.

10. Interview of Counts by author, December 21, 1962.

11. Counts, *The American Road to Culture* (New York: John Day Co., 1930), pp. 148–49.

12. Counts, *Social Foundations*, p. 277.

13. Ibid., p. 278.

14. Ibid., pp. 278–79.

15. Ibid.

16. George S. Counts, "A Proposal for Historical and Cultural Foundations at Columbia," in the private library of George S. Counts, Carbondale, Illinois, p. 1.

17. Counts, *Educacao para uma sociedade de homens livres na era technologica* (Rio de Janeiro: Centro Brasiliero de Pesquisas educacionais, 1958), p. 71.

18. Counts, "Dare Progressive Education Be Progressive?" *Progressive Education* 9 (1932), 257–58.

19. "Notes on the Convention," *Progressive Education* 9 (1932), 288.

20. Merle Curti, *The Social Ideas of American Educators* (Paterson, N.J.: Littlefield, Adams & Co., 1959), pp. 571–72. Adolph E. Meyer, *The Development of Education in the Twentieth Century* (Englewood Cliffs, N.J.: Prentice-Hall, 1949), pp. 84–87. Lawrence A. Cremin, *The Transformation of the School* (New York: Alfred A. Knopf, 1961), pp. 259–60.

21. Counts, "Dare Progressive Education," p. 256.

22. Ibid., p. 259.

23. Counts, *Dare the Schools*, pp. 7–8.

24. **Ibid.**, pp. 8–9.

25. Counts, "Dare Progressive Education," p. 258.

26. Counts, *Dare the Schools*, pp. 23–24.

27. John L. Childs, *American Pragmatism and Education* (New York: Henry Holt & Co., 1956), p. 222.

28. Counts, *Dare the Schools*, pp. 24–25.

29. "Notes on the Convention," p. 289.

30. "The Association Faces its Opportunities," *Progressive Education*, 9 (1932), 229.

31. Cremin, *Transformation of School*, p. 262.

32. Committee of the Progressive Education Association on Social and Economic Problems, *A Call to the Teachers of the Nation* (New York: John Day Co., 1933), p. 5.

33. Ibid., p. 27.

34. Interview of Counts by author, December 21, 1962.

35. Childs, *American Pragmatism*, p. 216.

36. Counts, *Education and American Civilization*, p. 39.

37. *A Call to the Teachers*, p. 28.

38. Ibid., p. 27.

39. Ibid., pp. 27–28.

40. Ibid., p. 29.

41. "Orientation," *Social Frontier*, 1 (1934), 4.

42. "Collectivism and Collectivism," *Social Frontier*, 1 (1934), 4.

43. "Orientation," pp. 4–5.

44. "Education for Tomorrow," p. 7.

45. Meyer, *Development of Education*, pp. 89–90.

46. Curti, *Social Ideas*, p. xxxi.

47. "Unmentionable Counts," *Time*, 28 (July 20, 1936), 66–68.

48. *New York Times*, September 18, 1934.

49. *Indianapolis News*, September 22, 1934.

50. *Bridgeport* (Conn.) *Telegram*, September 18, 1934.

51. Robert Iversen, *The Communists and the Schools* (New York: Harcourt, Brace & Co., 1959), p. 64.

52. Counts, *The Soviet Challenge to America* (New York: John Day Co., 1931), p. 10.

53. Ibid., p. 304.

54. Ibid., p. 316.

55. Ibid., p. 42.

56. Ibid., p. 242.

57. Ibid., p. 4.

58. Counts, *The Prospects of American Democracy* (New York: John Day Co., 1938), pp. 3–4.

59. Counts, *The Schools Can Teach Democracy* (New York: John Day Co., 1939), p. 6.

60. Iversen, *The Communists*, p. 115.

61. John L. Childs and George S. Counts, *America, Russia, and the Communist Party in the Postwar World* (New York: John Day Co., 1943), pp. 86–87.

62. B. P. Yesipov and N. K. Goncharov, *I Want to be Like Stalin*, tr. George S. Counts and Nucia P. Lodge (New York: John Day Co., 1947), pp. 13–14.

63. Ibid., p. 32.

64. Counts, *Education and American Civilization*, p. 16.

IV. Education and Democratic Collectivism

Counts's analysis of the American heritage devoted considerable attention to democracy and technology. These two elements constituted a major part of his frame of reference used to analyze American civilization. In addition to democracy and technology, economic conditioning served as the motive force in shaping the social and political contours of American society. In the light of his analysis of American democracy in an industrialized age, Counts concluded that the period of economic individualism was over and that of collectivism emergent. His primary purpose in analyzing American society was to formulate a viable concept of democracy upon which to base an educational philosophy and program.

Education and the Democratic Ideal

As he analyzed the American educational system, Counts found the democratic ideal expressed in several areas, such as in the creation of the free public school, the upward extension of educational opportunity, and the establishment of the single track system. Emphasizing the dignity and worth of the individual, equality of educational opportunity was theoretically open to all by reason of talents, efforts, and character. In his analysis of the democratic origins, Counts asserted that equality of condition produced economic, social, and political equality. Derived from these egalitarian moorings, the American educational system in both premise and genesis served the democratic heritage.

During the depression, Counts warned that the ascendancy of an "economic aristocracy" and the decline of effective political processes had weakened democracy's supporting structure. This threat to the democratic foundations also menaced democratic education. In fact, he found the contemporary struggle for democracy in the United States focused in the area of organized education. To preserve democracy, Counts called for a collectivistic economy to release the inventive and organizing energies of the people. He warned in *The Prospects of American Democracy* (1938) that unless the American people directed the school to serve democracy they could not possibly curb the ascendancy of the "economic aristocracy." The struggle between the aristocracy and the masses deeply involved education.[1] The American system of public education faced its supreme test in the current battle for democracy.

This struggle involved public education in the political arena since advocates of academic freedom, especially teachers, had a vested interest in the outcome of the battle. Under totalitarianism, freedom of inquiry and thought perished. In this crucial struggle, confusion reigned over fundamental issues such as indoctrination, freedom of teaching, and formulation of educational policies. These issues involved educators in politics whether they liked it or not. To clarify the field of the coming struggle, Counts analyzed three conflicting conceptions of the relationships between education and politics: education as separate from politics; education as an instrument of politics; and education as a force in politics.

The concept of education as separate from politics suggested the complete isolation of education from political life. To the extent that outside pressures infringed on the educational program, the school was violated and corrupted. According to this view, education molded the mind through mastery of universal and abiding tools, forms, and categories of human thought and experience. This conception did not include solution of current social problems.[2] Since Counts conceived education as conditioned by a particular concept of civilization at a specific time, the isolation of the school from social and political life falsified the educational function. Accordingly, Counts rejected a concept of education operating in isolation from society.

Opposing the concept of education as isolated from politics was a view of education as an instrument of politics. According to this concept, education functioned as a mere political tool. As an organ of the state, party, or class, education guided the program of the dominant group to fruition. Of itself, the school fulfilled only a secondary role in the social process.[3] Counts's analysis of American society indicated that the dominant class, the economic aristocracy, used the school as such a tool. Obviously, Counts rejected the use of the school as a puppet as inconsistent with the democratic ideal.

The third concept of education conceived the school as a social and political force. From this viewpoint, education existed as an original and creative force in civilization. Although produced by a particular set of historical and geographical relations and always local, temporal, and transitory, education possessed integrity. Although revealing the impress of a particular society in purpose, content, and method, education was not bound completely by the existent balance of social forces. Escaping the viciousness of economic, political, and historical determinism, education could intervene in the struggle of forces seeking social control. Although limited in its powers, Counts asserted that education could build a new social order.[4] In _The Schools Can Teach Democracy_ (1939) Counts stated that the public school had a significant role in the defense and advance of democracy. Accordingly, he repudiated the concepts of education as isolated from social values and systems and that of education as the tool of the dominant class. In rejecting social and moral neutrality, he urged education to promote the democratic tradition and way of life.[5]

Old Civic Education Unsuited to the Emergent Age

To the unwary and uncritical, it might seem that Counts's arguments for a committed philosophy and program of education were unnecessary. To these observers, the American system of publicly supported education had always advanced democracy by inculcating the democratic heritage as a part of civic education. In _The American Road to Culture_ (1930) Counts examined the nature of civic education and found Americans traditionally concerned with social solidarity. The loose organization of frontier life aroused a natural concern for unity and patriotism. The vastness of the country, ethnic heterogeneity, and relative weakness of an ingrained social tradition made imperative the creation of a common national identity. The creation of the common school and compulsory educational requirements partially satisfied this need.[6] Counts found that national solidarity rested on a foundation of common ideas, beliefs, sentiments, and loyalties inculcated through the common school program.

In addition to cementing social and political cohesiveness, civic education was a vehicle of patriotism. Stressing battles won by American heroes, this education sometimes produced an unquestioning patriotism bordering on chauvinism. Often appearing as a collection of patriotic slogans, Counts stated that traditional civic education promoted an unswerving loyalty to the status quo.[7] This narrow conception of civic education was inadequate for the needs of an integrated, complex, technological society. The ideal of democratic collectivism, envisioned by Counts, could not be confined within the limits of a narrowly conceived patriotism.

For Counts, traditional civic education failed to produce citizens capable of understanding the emergent social order. Although literate, they lacked comprehension of what they read. Children learned formal aspects of government without recognizing the underlying economic and social forces. Traditional civic education failed to penetrate into American history, institutions, and society.[8] Counts urged public education to prepare the future generation to participate actively and courageously in building a democratic industrial society. Instead of selfish nationalism, this society was to cooperate with other nations in the exchange of goods, cultivation of the arts, and advancement of knowledge, thought, and preservation of world peace.[9] For Counts, a truly democratic concept of education could no longer rely on homely slogans and patriotic platitudes but rather had to involve itself in the real struggles for democracy in the economic, social, and political world. Not isolated from reality nor a pawn of aristocracy, true civic education needed commitment to a definite program designed to fortify, preserve, and advance popular government through the democratic processes within the contours of industrialized society.

Educational Program Must Be Committed to an Ideology

In his criticism of traditional civic education, Counts stated that this outmoded educational program lacked any great ideal capable of enlisting the loyalties and disciplining the energies of youth. In response to the problems of cultural transition and economic depression, Counts called for a theory and program of education which incorporated a social philosophy adequate to the national tasks. Such a philosophy, he said, needed substance, form, and the incorporation of great historic choices. It had to be specifically suited to the needs of American civilization at a particular time and place in history.[10] Calling upon educators to reject neutrality and impartiality, Counts stated that any concrete educational program must contribute to the struggle among institutions, ideas, and values. As partiality and commitment were the essences of life, so were they the essences of education. The school could not remain neutral in any final and complete sense.[11]

Counts urged the educational profession to fashion a democratic program and philosophy of education. Although limited in ability to generate democratic reconstruction, the school and the teacher could no longer rely on direction from outside the educational milieu. Teachers had to formulate social ends directed to the democratic commitment and meet the needs posed by the rapidly changing technological society.[12]

In outlining a democratic program of education, Counts emphasized two major sets of objectives: One, development of democratic habits, dispositions, and loyalties; two, acquisition of knowledge and insight for intelligent participation in democratic society. By incorporating a pattern of democratic living, public education was to strive to develop a feeling of competence and adequacy in the individual; allegiance to human equality, brotherhood, dignity, and worth; loyalty to the democratic methodology of discussion, criticism, and decision; a mentality characterized by integrity and scientific spirit; respect for talent, training, and character. Finally, a sense of social obligation and devotion to the common good were prized hallmarks in the value pattern of democratic life.[13]

Counts urged the school to tell the story of American democracy in meaningful terms by relating it to the current social and political struggles. No longer relying on platitudes and patriotic jingles, the school was to lead students to critically examine the American heritage. In outlining the program of democratic education, Counts advocated the consideration of the origins of Western civilization and world history in its economic, social, cultural, and political aspects. This critical analysis of civilization included the ethical teachings of Judaism and Christianity, a study of the decline of feudalism, frontier influences, the preindustrial agrarian economy, the abolition of Negro slavery, accounts of the immigration of the underprivileged and oppressed of other lands, and the rise of organizations of workingmen. He also urged the survey of the equalitarian and democratic social ideas of the Enlightenment, the Declaration of Independence, popular government, separation of church and state, public education, and the advance of civil rights.[14] This broad program not only considered the achievements and origins of American civilization, but it also presented a survey of the threats and dangers which menaced democracy. Counts recommended the critical investigation of the passing of the frontier and agrarian orders, the development of commercial, industrial, and finance capitalism, concentration of economic power and emergence of plutocracy, and the attacks on democracy at home and abroad.[15]

Counts's call for an educational program committed to democracy presented a challenge to education. Both the scope and penetration of the outlined program demanded specially trained and competent teachers. He suggested a great bulk of sociological, historical, economic, and political materials. The mere listing of topics did not constitute a comprehensive educational program fitted to the preservation of democracy. This material needed careful organization according to a selective criteria. In evaluating the suggested program of democratic education, Counts stressed the spirit of the program rather than the organization or the methodological approach.

Counts's proposed program of democratic education differed radically from the old form of civic education which stressed national solidarity and patriotism and only superficially treated the history, politics, society, and economics of the American heritage. At this point, it is sufficient to state that Counts advocated a form of education committed to a concept of democratic collectivism. A more detailed discussion of the nature of this commitment will follow.

Education and Technology

Counts found technology a major component of American civilization. The industrial revolution, aided by science and invention, transformed man's material world. A cultural lag developed as man's reconstruction of his nonmaterial systems of morals, politics, laws, and institutions fell behind the material advances wrought by the technological revolution. The forms, practices, and institutions of American education, too, were caught up in this cultural lag. As Counts asserted many times, man's survival in the modern world was a race between disaster and education. Technology, therefore, had great importance for education.

Industrialism created a society of enormous complexity, characterized by specialization and multiplication of occupations. In the old agrarian economy, knowledge and experience necessary for managing farm and community were gained immediately and directly through the ordinary and actual processes of living and working. No longer true in the specialized, integrated, and complicated industrial order, the knowledge and experience appropriate to industrial society were increasingly gained through the more systematic methods of formally organized educational agencies. Thus, as industrial society provided new occupational opportunities, the task of training devolved upon the school. The growth of educational institutions and opportunities increased with the advancing industrial order and were intimately connected with technology.[16]

To Counts, the existence of vast interdependence, collectivism, and increased government participation related to the emergence of the technological order required a more social, cooperative, and integrated morality. Unfortunately, American education failed to aid in the building of this social intelligence and morality. Instead of a collectivistic value orientation, American education still promoted the competitive social morality associated with the legacy of economic individualism. To correct this fault, Counts urged that the technological foundations of modern American society be subjected to systematic instruction and critical examination in the pubilc schools. The educational program was to center on the scientific method and mathematical processes. In terms of general education, Counts stressed the method, ways of thought, and general impact of science on the life and condition of man. He asserted that the rising generation should be brought to a realization of science as a powerful instrument for understanding, subduing, and harnessing the forces of nature.

As Counts had advocated a systematic study of the origins and problems of democracy, he also urged a careful examination of the rise of industrial society. Education should indicate, he said, how science and technology, within the capitalistic matrix, had gradually transformed the economic and underlying conditions of life. He charged the school with analyzing the new forms of production and exchange, the increased role of capital goods, changed conditions of warfare, the expanded range of communications and markets, new class divisions and conflicts, the need for planning and control, and the social, political, and economic maladjustments associated with the new economic age.[17]

Counts directly related the proposed program of education for a technological civilization to economics. Any program of education which examined technological and industrialized society was necessarily concerned with the economic basis of modern society. American education had come to stress economic efficiency, division of labor, and skilled training for differentiated occupations. While American education stressed technology in a limited and superficial sense, Counts advocated a more broadened, humane, and penetrating study of technology than mere vocational training to supply skilled workers. Thus, he urged a more radical departure in the area of technological education than hitherto practiced. He found the problems of education in American democracy intertwined with technology. Although for purposes of analysis these two

areas have been separated, their close integration constituted
a basic core or cluster of related problems.

Economics and Education

Economic conditioning constituted a major element in
Counts's analysis of American society and education during
the depression period. He traced many of the conflicts in
American society to traditional economic individualism which
governed both school and society. To Counts, a reconstructed
economy, based upon a form of democratic collectivism, was
needed to preserve American democracy against the attacks of
the economic aristocracy. Counts's emphasis on economics
brought him into controversy with another noted American
educator, Boyd H. Bode. In 1935, the pages of *Social Frontier*,
edited by Counts, carried the attack of Bode on Counts's analysis and Counts's defense of the economic emphasis. A mention
of this controversy illustrates the importance which Counts
attached to the economic role in formulating a philosophy of
education designed to build a new social order in the midst of
cultural transition and economic depression.

Neither Bode nor Counts were attached to the traditional
education, and both educators were among the group of like-
minded Progressives. However, Bode challenged the thesis
advanced in *Social Frontier* that economic reconstruction was
preliminary to reconstruction in other areas of life. Bode
charged that the editors, Counts and his associates, Woelfel
and Grossman, assumed that the need for reconstruction in
other areas was not as pressing as the need for economic and
industrial reconstruction. The editors, he alleged, believed that
the domains of cultural, religious, and social life had to wait

until the recasting of the economic order. Claiming that *Social Frontier* was too conservative, Bode asked what justification the editors had for ignoring the real and significant breakdown of the cultural, religious, and social patterns.[18]

Bode dissented from a thesis that placed economic values above all others. He urged that any attempt at social reconstruction should include consideration of cultural, aesthetic, and intellectual values as well as economic ones. By stressing economic values and ignoring other values, Bode warned that attempted reconstruction invited some form of dictatorship: "How can we hope to humanize industry and make it a means for the realization of spiritual values, as long as we propose to do the reconstructing first and to take up the question of these other values afterwards?" [19]

As an alternative to economic conditioning, Bode urged a genuine program of reconstruction which did not predetermine conclusions. Extensive economic reconstruction, he alleged, was limited as long as traditional social, cultural, and political modes remained untouched. He continued, education needed a broader outlook and the direction of energies to the reconstruction of all basic life patterns. Finally, he charged that *Social Frontier*'s aggressive attacks against the existent economic order concealed the lack of a comprehensive educational philosophy and program.[20]

Counts, and his associate editors, rose to Bode's challenge. They stated that economics conditioned all life. History indicated that politics, philosophy, morals, class, and social relationships were conditioned by changing methods of creating and distributing wealth. Relating their reply to the depression, the editors stated that during periods of economic insecurity life lacked stability in the noneconomic areas. Alternating periods of overwork and unemployment sapped the physical and intellectual vitality of people; where profit dominated, art lacked intrinsic considerations and corruption dominated political life; an artificially produced scarcity frustrated science. Finally, they stated that where inherited economic patterns were unstable and irrational, the beneficiaries of these patterns would not permit analysis, criticism, experimentation, and reasoning about social matters.[21]

After defending economic conditioning, Counts and his associates turned specifically to Bode's challenges. First, they defended their economic emphasis by stating that reconstruction of economic life was basic to reconstruction of other areas of life. Bode, they said, misconstrued the editor's position by asserting that *Social Frontier* aimed at the reconstruction of the industrial life and economic life as preliminary to other areas. To the editors, reconstruction of economic life was essential rather than preliminary to the transformation of life as a whole. They agreed with Bode that all aspects of institutional life should be reconstructed. However, their differences with Bode were not a matter of goals but rather of strategy.[22]

Secondly, the editors of *Social Frontier* asserted a belief in directed reconstruction, while Bode, they said, advocated undirected reconstruction. They charged that Bode urged a program of social reconstruction without specifying criteria that the reconstructed patterns of life had to meet. The editors cautioned Bode that an undirected reconstruction was not genuinely reconstructive. A scheme of education limited merely to criticism was ineffective. The editors affirmed their policy by stating: "We are committed to the fashioning of such attitudes, ideas, and ideals and to the crystallization of affiliation with such groups as can best be expected to create the new life." [23]

In meeting Bode's attacks on his emphasis on economic conditioning, Counts defended his argument that the economic bases of American society should be examined carefully. During the 1930s economic conditioning was a major element in Counts's social and political analysis of the American heritage. It also exercised a major role in the formulation of an educational program designed to build a new social order. After defending economic conditioning in the formulation of a reconstructive philosophy and program, Counts outlined two alternative programs of education. Education could proceed either in a society dominated by an economic aristocracy or it could occur in a society characterized by democratic collectivism.

Education Under an Economic Aristocracy

Counts warned that a small minority had gained title to most of the productive property of the nation as technology drove economic organization into collective patterns. The great historical choice before the American people was that of using this collective energy in either minority or majority interests. If the collective economy served the economic aristocracy, then the masses would receive only enough goods and services to maintain them at an optimum working capacity. The vast amount of the social income would accrue to the aristocracy who would support a repressive police force and enjoy the luxuries produced by the toiling masses.[24]

If the economic elite prevailed, Counts further predicted the loss of the distinctive equalitarian nature of American education. A dual system of education would replace the single-track pattern. While part of the educational system served the privileged, the masses would attend lower and inferior educational institutions. The children of the ruling classes would attend special schools designed to instill a feeling of superiority and the language, manners, sports, and world view suited to a governing elite. The major function of the schools attended by the children of the aristocracy would be inculcation of the notion that their privileges and rank rested on providential or natural sanctions.

The children of the masses would attend the lower and inferior schools which provided limited education suitable to a servant caste. The primary function of the inferior school would be to inculcate in the minds of the children of the masses that they lived in the best of all possible worlds. Existing institutions, practices, distribution of wealth, income, power, privilege, and opportunity would be exalted as expressions of immutable natural laws. This school might also exercise a selective function under the domination of the aristocracy. Discontented or superior individuals could be detached from the masses and possibly raised into the privileged ranks.[25] Thus, Counts concluded, a society divided into rigidly stratified classes would foster an educational system which promoted continued stratification.

True to his egalitarian bias, Counts urged educators to resist the domination of the economic aristocracy over American schools. In his analysis of American society, he postulated a plan of political action designed to block the domination of the nation by an elite. In the long run, however, a social philosophy based upon democratic collectivism and promoted by organized education would best offset the growth of the aristocracy, or at least be a valuable addition to political action. Counts urged commitment of organized education to the popular masses in the struggle to control the productive capacity of a collectivized economic order. Counts stated that in this power struggle the aristocracy benefited by the retention of the inherited social system based on economic individualism, ruthless competition, and social and cultural stratification. On the other hand, the popular masses profited by collective ownership and management of the economy, social planning of production and distribution, and the substitution of the motive of social utility for that of private profit. Counts stated that the school had to make a choice in the struggle and could not long remain neutral:

> Between these two ways of living there can be no real and lasting compromise. Between these two groups, one of which lives through the exploitation of the other, there can be no real and lasting peace. The choice before the school is not between taking sides in the conflict and remaining above the battle in the stratosphere of objective fact and pure reason, but rather between taking sides vigorously and placing itself outside the realm of everything that is really vital, important, and significant today.[26]

Commitment to Democratic Collectivism

For Counts, emergent collectivism constituted a great historic trend that educators had to recognize. In his social analysis, he asserted that the survival of American democracy required the abandonment of economic individualism. After divorcing technology from social privilege, Counts urged that the resulting productive and distributive system directly serve the popular masses. The democratic tradition must expand to assume an essentially collective pattern.[27] Guided by the emergent economic collectivism, the controlling purpose of the American school required radical revision. Counts stated that the school could not escape this fundamental reality in formulating an educational program capable of serving contemporary society.[28]

Counts stated that the program of public education was to equip the younger generation for labor and sacrifice in building a democratic civilization and culture on the foundations of a collective economy. The commitment of the educational program to democratic collectivism required abandonment of many inherited educational customs and practices. For example, the old educational tradition regarded the school as the road to special privilege and preferred occupational status. The new education aimed to abolish all artificial social distinctions and to organize the national energies for social improvement. While competition dominated the old educational program, the new would emphasize collectivism and cooperation based on the spirit of social obligation. For Counts, a spirit promising the fullest utilization of human resources in advancing the general welfare governed the educational program of democratic collectivism.[29] Reflecting this view, the Committee of the Progressive Education Association on Social and Economic Problems urged a collectivistic philosophy of education in *A Call To the Teachers of the Nation* in 1933:

> Our philosophy of education should be securely rooted in the democratic-revolutionary tradition of the American people, but should bathe its branches in the atmosphere of industrial civilization and the world of nations. It should aim to foster in boys and girls a profound sense of human worth, a genuine devotion to the welfare of the masses, a deep aversion to the tyranny of privilege, warm feeling of kinship with all the races of mankind, and a quick readiness to engage in bold social experimentation.

It should also accept industrial society as an established fact, cease casting nostalgic eyes towards the agrarian past, take up boldly the challenge of the present, recognize the corporate and interdependent character of the contemporary order, and transfer the democratic tradition from individualistic to collectivistic economic foundations.[30]

Democracy and Technology in the Post–World War II Era

Democracy and technology constituted two of the prevailing elements of Counts's theory of both American civilization and of an educational philosophy designed for that particular civilization. His later works minimized democratic collectivism and stressed a broadened education for democracy emphasizing two factors: one, a clear recognition of the democratic foundations of American society; two, the role of decision-making by ordinary citizens in a democracy.

Both *Education and the Promise of America* (1946) and *Education and American Civilization* (1952) urged that educational programs clarify the foundations of political liberty in the United States. Counts advocated the organization and conduct of the entire educational program for the development of the qualities and powers essential to perpetuating a free society. As one of the first obligations of the school, he urged the study of the dangers to political liberty.[31] He still advocated the formulation of a historic concept of democracy to guide the entire educational enterprise. Counts stated that American youth lacked a great ideal capable of enlisting loyalty and disciplining energies to constructive purposes. He reminded that each generation needed an abiding affection, devotion, and faith in their native land. This task could be achieved by actively and intelligently identifying devotion to country with the overriding purpose of the American heritage. He also stated that the national state was the stubborn reality of the age. Achievement of a peaceful and comprehensive international organization could come only through the national states and not some nebulous body of internationalists.[32]

Although at first glance it seemed that he reverted to the old civic education which he condemned during the 1930s, Counts rather advocated loyalty to the nation which embodied a sense of democratic mission. He had always objected to cynicism and lack of purpose which he believed sapped energy and aim. To develop habits, dispositions, and loyalties of free people in the young, American education needed to reaffirm the democratic commitment.

As the second major facet of democratic education, Counts advocated the forthright study of the great issues of government and civilization. In *Education and the Foundations of Human Freedom* (1962) he stated that the education of free men must emphasize relevant knowledge and understanding. He found American society victimized by anti-intellectual traditions. For the triumph of freedom over despotism, these tendencies had to be negated and the intellectual stature of American citizens increased. To accomplish this, educational institutions had to convey an understanding of the American political system and the foundations of human freedom. The following great challenges presented by the age needed analysis and exposition: communism and other forms of totalitarianism, the decline of the West and rise of non-Western peoples, and the challenge of the complexity and dynamism of society and culture.[33]

Counts's views of the problems of democracy in the post–

World War II era indicated concern with the increased complexity of the world and the nation. His plea for increased investigation of the foundations of human freedom revealed a realization of the complex problems involved in carrying on the democratic processes in the modern world. Despite the immensity of the task, Counts still believed the ordinary American citizen capable of fulfilling the requirements of the democratic process. His later analyses focused on world issues and foreign challenges to democracy. Counts reflected the shift that characterized the American social and educational scene as problems changed from the domestic to the international area.

In his works of the 1940s and 1950s, Counts continued to emphasize technology, the second basic supporting element in his analysis of modern American civilization. Although the mastery and advance of scientific and technical knowledge was an obvious problem, the crucial problems existed in the social, political, and moral spheres—in the area of values and understanding. Counts urged American education to strive to rear a generation capable of living with and directing toward humane ends all the resources of science and technology.[34] In *Education and the Promise of America* (1946), Counts urged that the educational program acquaint the young with basic technological patterns. This was not another form of vocational training in the narrow sense but was to convey understandings and shape dispositions. Counts stated that education had not deliberately incorporated these new industrial elements into civilization and had permitted an aversion toward technology.[35] Counts always advocated a broad and humane understanding of science and technology, which he viewed as instruments of great cultural significance rather than as narrow methodological instruments for performing certain restrictive operations.

Counts urged organized education to provide for the acquaintance of the young with the vast range of occupational opportunities in industrial society. A comprehensive program of vocational training should be undertaken, embracing all important occupations, and available to all. He also recommended a program of genuine work experience under conditions of production and market to avoid isolating the school from life.[36] Like Dewey, Counts rejected a specific vocational training that forced the recipient into a fixed routine from which there were slight opportunities for growth. Both Dewey and Counts conceived of vocational education as continuous activity which rendered service to others and engaged individual powers in accomplishing results. As Dewey stated, vocational education "would give those who engage in industrial callings desire and ability to share in social control, and ability to become masters of their industrial fate." [37]

In the light of this broadened view of vocational education, Counts urged education to alter the traditional view of stressing goods before services. Traditionally, the production of services was regarded as secondary to that of goods. Counts felt that this inherited conception of the capitalistic economy which stressed material goods was obsolete in the face of modern needs. He warned that as automation advanced the percentage of people engaged in production of material goods would decline. Achievement of full employment necessitated the move into the service occupations of health, education, science, recreation, entertainment, and the arts for the enrichment and refinement of personal and community life.[38]

Both *Education and the Promise of America* and *Educa-*

tion and American Civilization revealed Counts's continuing concern with economics, as he stated that industrial civilization offered the American people a life of material prosperity. It was technically possible to drive poverty, material privation, debasing toil, and economic insecurity from the land. Despite achievement of adequate production processes, methods of distribution remained inadequate. Counts restated his earlier message: "We need to devise an educationl program that will bring our people abreast of the material world in which they live and that will equip them to solve the many problems involved in building a stable and abundant economy." [39]

In *Education and American Civilization,* Counts stated that the foundations of a stable economy must be established since economic forces exercised a powerful role in human society. Since every truly great civilization required an adequate and stable material base, he continued, American democracy could endure only under conditions of economic security. Employment of educational resources was needed to facilitate economic security. He suggested a program of general economic education to include study of the system of institutions, relationships, and processes which sustained economic livelihood. Individuals were to realize the relation of their specialty to the whole of life. He further recommended that attention be given to consumer education and to the development of understanding of the role played by natural resources in economic life. [40] Counts's entire program of economic education focused on the integration and interdependency of economic life in modern society.

Throughout his social and educational writings, Counts urged increased efforts to effect a deliberate and rationally planned integration and coordination of the economy. For him, the central problem remained that of achieving coordination

among the various branches of the economy and between production and consumption to prevent economic crises and depressions; this, he believed, would insure a steady advance in
the living standards of all people. Educational policies were
to further this desired coordination. He found educational efforts needed to achieve a synthesis of moral values embracing
both old and new elements which emphasized the worth of
socially useful labor. The development of cooperative attitudes
and practices constituted another urgent educational task in
an industrial economy.[41] Thus, Counts's works continued to
relate educational policy to economic conditions. However,
the sense of urgency voiced during the 1930s ebbed as the economic crisis subsided. In these works, he recommended educational policies designed to forestall any repetition of the events
of the depression era.

Education for Democratic Collectivism Evaluated

In his social analysis, Counts treated the key elements of
the American heritage, democracy and technology. After tracing in detail the rise of American democracy and of industrialized technological society, Counts's solutions failed to match
the boldness of the inquiry. Instead of advocating the definite
steps necessary for achieving democratic collectivism, Counts
recommended reliance on the processes of political democracy
and experimentalism. In his educational theory, he called for
a philosophy and program to further democratic collectivism.
Instead of recommending a precise educational program,
Counts exposed an orientation appropriate to democracy in
a collectivistic society. He urged the study of and analysis by
the school of both democracy and collectivism, the elimination

of laissez faire attitudes, and the cultivation of cooperative values in the schools. He also defended his predilection to economic conditioning in the formulation of educational policies against his critics.

Counts's formulation of a philosophy and program of education to advance democratic collectivism contained a large amount of generality. He failed to indicate the steps necessary in formulating the democratic collectivist educational philosophy. On the other hand, critics such as Bode accused him of having predetermined the educational ends. It seems that if any charge against Counts was valid it was that of being too vague rather than of being too precise. Once again using the experimentalist methodology, educators were to fashion the educational program. Despite the great amount of freedom which they were given by Counts, educators were to frame their operations within the general confines of the emergent pattern of the age, democratic collectivism. To more clearly exposit Counts's program of democratic collectivism, it is proposed to examine his plea for an educational program committed to imposition of this view of the cultural heritage. Therefore the next chapters will be concerned with the nature of imposition advocated by Counts, his proposed curriculum, the program of teacher education, and finally an over-all view of his educational program.

1. George S. Counts, *The Prospects of American Democracy* (New York: John Day Co., 1938), p. 290.

2. Ibid., p. 294.

3. Ibid., p. 295.

4. Ibid., pp. 294–95.

5. Counts, *The Schools Can Teach Democracy* (New York: John Day Co., 1939), pp. 15–16.

6. Counts, *The American Road to Culture* (New York: John Day Co., 1930), pp. 108–9.

7. Ibid., p. 117.

8. Counts, *Prospects,* pp. 248–49.

9. Counts, *The Social Foundations of Education* (New York: Charles Scribner's Sons, 1934), p. 544.

10. Ibid., p. 534.

11. Ibid., p. 535.

12. "The Position of the Social Frontier," *Social Frontier,* 1 (1935), 30–31.

13. Counts, *Schools Can Teach Democracy,* pp. 16–17.

14. Ibid., pp. 23–24.

15. Ibid.

16. Counts, "Selection as a Function of American Secondary Education," *National Education Association Proceedings,* 67 (1929), 600.

17. Counts, *Schools Can Teach Democracy,* p. 26.

18. Boyd H. Bode, "Dr. Bode Replies," *Social Frontier,* 2 (1935), 42.

19. Ibid., 43.

20. Ibid.

21. "Economics and the Good Life," *Social Frontier,* 2 (1935), 73.

22. Ibid., 72.

23. Ibid.

24. Counts, *Social Foundations,* p. 539.

25. Ibid., p. 540.

26. "Position of Social Frontier," 31.

27. Counts, "Education For What?" *New Republic,* 71 (1932), 40.

28. Counts, *Social Foundations,* pp. 538–39.

29. Ibid., p. 542.

30. Committee of the Progressive Education Association on Social

and Economic Problems, *A Call To the Teachers of the Nation* (New York, 1932), pp. 20–21.

31. Counts, *Education and American Civilization* (New York: Bureau of Publications, Teachers College, Columbia University, 1952), p. 354.

32. Ibid., p. 411.

33. Counts, *Education and the Foundations of Human Freedom* (Pittsburgh: University of Pittsburgh Press, 1962), pp. 84–85.

34. Counts, *Educacao para uma sociedade de homens livres na era tecnologica* (Rio de Janeiro: Centro Brasiliero de Pesquisas educacionais, 1958), pp. 77–78.

35. Counts, *Education and the Promise of America* (New York: Macmillan Co., 1946), pp. 131–32.

36. Ibid., pp. 132–33.

37. John Dewey, *Democracy and Education* (New York: Macmillan Co., 1916), p. 374.

38. Counts, *Education and the Promise,* p. 60.

39. Ibid., p. 130.

40. Counts, *Education and American Civilization,* pp. 374–75.

41. Ibid., p. 41.

V. The Nature of Imposition

Counts's analysis of the American cultural heritage convinced him that American civilization verged on a collectivistic age. In the spirit of the heritage, Counts urged the American educational profession to develop a philosophy and program which facilitated transition into the age of democratic collectivism. To accomplish this goal, Counts suggested that the American system of public education deliberately commit itself to advancing the necessary conditions and purposes. Motivated by democratic collectivism, he urged the school to deliberately impose this ideal. During the 1930s, in particular, Counts urged the acceptance of this idea of committed education. His advocacy of educational imposition resulted in controversy and debate. To clarify his position, Counts examined the traditional reluctance of American education to imposition and clarified the meaning of imposition for the educational profession.

Traditional American Education Opposed Imposition

Advocating imposition, Counts encountered opposition from the American educational tradition which rejected deliberate use of the school to inculcate political and religious doctrines and dogma. This tradition originated as the embryonic public elementary school system struggled to overcome sectarian domination which characterized much of education in New England. After long struggle, the American educational belief developed in secularized schools. With the sectarian diversity and pluralistic nature of American society, the separation of church and state and sect and school was a natural response to a practical problem. Thus, the school, to maintain neutrality in religious affairs, left religious indoctrination to the family and church. Drawing upon this early tradition associated with public elementary education, the American educational system theoretically disavowed all forms of indoctrination and imposition.

In *The American Road to Culture* (1930) Counts examined the superficiality of religious neutrality and found Americans steeped in religious traditions. In a community dominated by a particular religious domination, the particular sectarian view usually entered the school program as a matter of course. In a wider sense, Counts stated that the program of the American public school was everywhere religious. The Christian ethnic permeated instruction and supported a value schema identified with historical Christianity.[1] Despite this religious attitude, the American people genuinely believed their educational system free from sectarianism.

To Counts, the American people feared using the schools for any kind of indoctrination. When through civic education they inculcated ideas of national solidarity and patriotism, they did not feel that indoctrination occurred. American educators, generally, opposed indoctrination in the schools and defined indoctrination as the teaching of any attitude as fixed, final, and unchanging. This peculiar opposition to imposition derived from what many educators prized as objective science. Holding that science imparted a dynamic quality to modern life, they believed that the indoctrination of the child with a fixed set of beliefs rendered him unfit for life in the real and changing world. Since nothing was stable in the external environment, the individual should be mentally flexible, highly sensitive to change, and capable of making rapid adjustments.[2] Since the Darwinian revolution, educators had claimed objectivity in formulating educational theories.

The professed objectivity and freedom of the American system of public education received further impetus with the progressive education movement of the 1920s. In *Social Frontier,* Counts analyzed the attitude of the "new educator" of the "Twenties." For the progressive of that period, indoctrination deliberately shaped the minds and consciences of students and rendered them dupes and instruments of those in power positions. In contrast to indoctrination, Counts stated, the typical progressive believed in a process of direct experience which led the student to formulate his own philosophy of life, social orientation, morality, and loyalties. To the progressive, indoctrination taught what to think while education taught how to think. Counts asserted that the typical progressive failed to distinguish between the various contents of the various indoctrinations but rather condemned all imposition.[3] During the period of the 1920s many progressive educators attempted to rid the schools of reactionary indoctrination in order to produce a generation of socially thoughtful men and women capable of reconstructing social life.[4] These advocates of extreme freedom championed child rights and rejected any molding of the learner. Thus, Counts found that American public education since its origin had opposed indoctrination. Conservative as well as progressive educators advocated a philosophy and program that was objective, impartial, and neutral.

All Education Is Biased

To persuade the American educational profession to undertake a program of education committed to democratic collectivism, Counts argued that all education involved imposition or indoctrination. Some criteria which aided in selection and rejection of goals, purposes, subjects, materials, and methods guided those in charge of the educational program. In these matters, education involved positive action and decision. At no point could the school assume complete neutrality and at the same time become a concrete, functioning reality. Counts stated that since education was concerned with a growing organism, growth needed direction. The determination of this direction constituted one of the greatest educational problems.[5]

Counts emphasized that no educational program was unbiased since every educational program had form and substance, pattern and value, aversion and loyalty. He stated that there existed an appropriate and distinctive education for every social order. The first obligation of American educators was clarification of the underlying assumptions and guiding principles which gave structure and direction to the school.[6] Such an obligation required a definite commitment to the values and conditions present in the American democratic heritage.

In rejecting social and moral neutrality, Counts urged the direction of the energies of organized education to the defense and strengthening of the democratic ethic. The crisis of cultural transition and economic depression demanded a great ideal capable of inspiring youth. If the tradition was vital and suited to the times, imposition released energies, established standards of excellence, and facilitated achievement.[7]

In his well-known work, *Dare the Schools Build a New Social Order?* (1932), Counts presented his arguments for an educational program committed to the imposition of democratic collectivism. He based his arguments for imposition on a refutation of the tenets of the new or progressive education which advocated educational neutralism: one, man was born free; two, the child was naturally good; three, the child lived in his own separate world; and four, the school should remain impartial.

Counts termed it fallacious to state that man was born free when he was actually born helpless. At birth, the child was a bundle of raw potentialities capable of development in any number of directions. Man achieved freedom, as individual and as a member of the race, through the mediation of a particular culture. "By being nurtured on a body of culture, however backward and limited it may be comparatively, the individual is at once imposed on and liberated." [8]

Through the medium of a particular culture, the child acquired language, meanings, traditions, and values. The culture was instrumental and practical as a body of tools, inventions, practices, folkways, customs, institutions, knowledges, and ideas on which depended the survival and perpetuation of society. The transmission of this stock of cultural possessions and the introduction of the immature to their use constituted a major educational function.[9] By this very act of inducting the young in the cultural heritage, education imposed a particular culture upon the young.

Counts believed that the culture served as an expression and repository of the hopes, aspirations, and values of a people. To this aspect of culture, which was integrative, directive, dynamic, and qualitative, the term tradition was applied. In choosing the appropriate tradition to impose, the most severe educational controversies arose. In this area, warned Counts, the question of imposition and indoctrination assumed acute form.[10]

In imposing a particular cultural heritage upon the immature, the group always made the choice. Counts stated that the survival of any human society depended on education as the particular society used the formative influences of education as a means of self-perpetuation. Cultural evolution would be impossible if the achievements of one generation were not transmitted to the next by the processes of teaching and learning. Each new generation inducted into the life of the group mastered inherited skills, knowledge, and philosophies. Without this transmission and imposition, the particular society perished.[11] Release of human energy occurred, not by freeing the individual from tradition but by inducing him to identify completely with a vital and growing tradition and find life fulfillment within that tradition. Life became integrated and effective only as the individual was influenced and nurtured by some particular tradition.[12] Without such a tradition, the condition of freedom was that of mediocrity, incompetence, and aimlessness. Counts concluded:

> The real question, therefore, is not whether some tradition will be imposed by intent or circumstance upon the coming generation (we may rest assured that this

will be done), but rather what particular tradition will
be imposed. To refuse to face the task of the selection
or the fashioning of this tradition is to evade the most
crucial, difficult, and important educational responsibility.[13]

By stressing the crucial importance of cultural imposition
for education, Counts came to the purpose of his analysis of
the American cultural heritage. By isolating and analyzing
the key elements of democracy and technology and by emphasizing the economic role in bringing about a collective society, Counts reached what he believed to be a viable concept
of American civilization, democratic collectivism. An educational profession committed to this concept could advance the
new social order by transmitting the goals and instruments
needed to construct the emergent society.

After disposing of the first fallacy, Counts turned to the
second which stated that the child was naturally good. Using
evidence from anthropology and observation, he stated that
at birth the individual was neither good nor bad. The progressive advocates of the new learning constructed their instructional program on the laws of child growth and development.
Although he found these laws of maturation and development extremely significant in the learning process, Counts
did not believe the guiding educational principles existed in
the study of the child's nature. Once again, this guidance derived from the group and the cultural heritage. Counts asserted "there can be no good individual apart from some conception of the character of the good society; and the good
society is not something that is given by nature: it must be
fashioned by the hand and brain of man." [14]

For Counts, as the native culture molded the individual,

the learning processes were also culturally influenced. He found the complete impartiality recommended by the critics of imposition an impossibility. The school shaped attitudes, developed tastes, and even imposed ideas. Since the school could not absorb the whole culture, some selective criteria guided selection of teachers, curricula, architecture, and methods. Referring to Dewey's admonition in *Democracy and Education* that the school was to provide a "purified environment," Counts stated that a purified environment demanded selection.[15] Although the nature of the child was truly significant in fashioning the learning program, it could not alone furnish the materials and guiding principles of that program. Education had to view the cultural heritage and the current social scene to fashion a philosophy and program of education. In addressing the convention of the Progressive Education Association in 1932, Counts stated: "if life were peaceful and quiet and undisturbed by great issues, we might, with some show of wisdom, center our attention on the nature of the child. But with the world as it is, we cannot afford for a single instant to remove our eyes from the social scene." [16]

Counts next turned to the third fallacy which he associated with progressive education, the child lived in a separate world of his own. Advocates of extreme child freedom considered the adult as an alien intruder in the child's life. Counts felt that this separation of the child from adult society created an artificial dualism. Whatever the child's view of the adult, both adult and child shared the same society. In a proper kind of society, the adult-child relationship was one of mutual benefit in which the young repaid in trust and emulation the protection and guidance provided by the elders.[17]

Finding the development of critical intelligence related to the maturation of the child, the school's program was graduated according to varying levels of maturity. Counts found much of the debate over the degree of freedom extended to the individual learner stemmed from a failure to delimit the particular age under consideration. He stated that the extent of guidance provided by the older and more expert members of the group varied inversely as the degree of maturity of the individual. For example, the kindergarden required much more adult intervention than the graduate college of the university.[18]

Counts also found that the advocates of extreme child freedom had been confused by certain historical causes. The champions of extreme child freedom themselves were products of an age that had only very recently parted with the past and was still uncertain as to the future. Many felt themselves victims of narrow orthodoxies imposed during childhood. At any suggestion that the child be influenced by adults, these proponents of extreme child freedom conjured up ghosts of the established state church and fixed social and religious dogmas. Counts stated that the choice was not limited to an unenlightened indoctrination or complete freedom.[19] An intelligent resolution of the controversy between a definite social orientation and complete child freedom did not point to either extreme.

Finally, Counts turned to one of the dangers which Dewey warned against in *Democracy and Education,* the isolation of school from society. By being isolated in a child's world, the developing individual became increasingly separated from serious life activities. In the United States with the spread of urban and industrial life, the child was increasingly separated from socially significant adult activities. Carefully protected from industry, the home provided scant activity. Counts charged that even in the progressive schools the child's activities lacked social significance.[20] Although some observers believed that the child's isolation was an inevitable corollary of the growing complexity of the modern social order, Counts challenged this view:

> In my opinion it is rather the product of a society that is moved by no great commanding ideals and is consequently victimized by the most terrible form of human madness—the struggle for private gain. Until school and society are bound together by common purposes the program of education will lack both meaning and vitality.[21]

Counts also directed attention to the most prevalent of the fallacies supporting educational neutrality—the school as completely impartial and unbiased in instruction. As a force in shaping and molding the individual along cultural lines, complete educational impartiality was impossible. Once again Counts referred to Dewey's special function of organized education as a purifying agency. To purify environment, Counts stated, some selective criteria had to be used which favored a particular value system. Finding it untenable that the program of education be confined to a purely objective description of social life, he stated that to function in society the school needed a definite social orientation. Genuinely effective schools had to become centers for the building of civilization and not for mere contemplation.[22] In urging a democratic orientation to the question of imposition, Counts stated:

> I believe firmly that democratic sentiments should be cultivated and that a better and richer life should be the outcome of education, but in neither case would I place responsibility on either God or the order of nature. I

would merely contend that as educators we must make choices involving the development of attitudes in boys and girls and that we should not be afraid to acknowledge the faith that is in us or the forces that compel us.[23]

Open-endedness and Committed Education

During the 1930s Counts gained eminence as a leading educational theorist. Although his collectivistic social orientation pointed to new directions, it was not unique to Counts during the depression period. Rather, his address before the Progressive Education Association and his later publication *Dare the School Build a New Social Order?* (1932) startled the educational profession by advancing the theory of deliberate imposition. Not only was Counts criticized by traditionalists for his reconstructionist views, he also aroused controversy within the community of progressive educators. Although the progressive community contained many reformist theorists, some of these also disagreed with Counts's attitudes on imposition. Although Counts's criticisms of progressive education have already been considered in the earlier chapter of this paper dealing with educational responses to the 1930s, some of the criticism directed by progressives against Counts has been reserved for this section on imposition.

Among the progressive educators who quarreled with Counts on the issue of indoctrination was Elsie R. Clapp. Counts, she said, was too vague in his suggestions on imposition. She questioned, did Counts advocate social change or was he prescribing an educational methodology? In her mind, these were two very different items. It was one thing to state that conditions should be different and quite another to recom-

mend a certain method of altering them. To her, indoctrination implied that a deliberately planned and executed procedure be undertaken to effect this deliberate alteration. Counts,
she warned, had obscured the lines between force, imposition,
training, instruction, and education. Returning to old progressive canons, she said that Counts neglected the nature of
the child and stressed the influence of adults and adult conditions.[24]

Ellen Geer, another progressive pioneer, joined the attack
on imposition. Instead of emphasizing the nature of the child,
she advanced a plea for "open-mindedness." In attacking
Counts's pleas for the building of a new social order, she stated
that it was uncertain that progressive educators had the wisdom to determine which of the many new social doctrines
would be the salvation of the world. She warned against per-
mitting the advocates of a social panacea to indoctrinate the
impressionable minds of children. Instead, she urged progressives to remain faithful to the theory of "open-mindedness."

> Shall we indoctrinate them with social theories which
> seem sound to us today, but which, by the time our chil-
> dren are able to accomplish anything for their further-
> ance, may be hopelessly outdated, and the adherence to
> which, will have incapacitated them for open-minded
> recognition of that fact?[25]

In an article entitled "The Teacher in Politics," Henry W.
Holmes continued the attack upon the imposition theory of
Counts. He quarreled with Counts on three major points:
one, indoctrination; two, political action on the part of teachers; and three, involvement of the school in social controver-

sies. Echoing the Cassandra-like warnings of the preceding educators, Holmes asserted that indoctrination actually denoted an effort to obtain a prejudiced, unreflecting, uncritical acceptance of a point of view, idea, or program. Connoting propaganda, it appealed to the emotions, self-interest, or bias.[26] In dealing with politics, Holmes cautioned teachers to be neither subversive nor reactionary. With respect to proposals for social change, it was the duty of the teachers to be clear, impartial, and as objective as possible. In maintaining a neutral attitude, he urged school authorities to handle controversial problems scrupulously. Finally, Holmes charged that Counts was not explicit as to how schools were to approach controversial issues. As public officers, Holmes said, teachers could not impose upon their pupils ideals or principles which were anathema to the majority of the population.[27]

In response to the criticism of the "child-centered" progressives, Counts replied that a large measure of imposition did not mean severe regimentation, or the rigorous teaching of fixed and final doctrine. Counts agreed that in the light of the highly dynamic social order of the modern world this kind of imposition would be extremely dangerous. Although he encouraged the child to question all things, this did not imply that a particular education program had to lack great social ideals.[28] Although convinced that the schools should communicate a definite orientation to democratic collectivism, this was not to be accomplished through deliberate distortion or suppression of facts.

On the basis of the criticisms levied against Counts, it seems that he had to tread a delicate course. If he indicated precisely the patterns to be followed, he was accused of violating the "open-endedness" of the instrumentalist methodology by foisting predetermined ends upon the school. On the other hand, if he was cautious in prescribing the course to be followed, he was attacked for being too vague and for failing to precisely delineate his program of democratic collectivism.

In the midst of the problems of the depression period of the 1930s, Counts's pleas for educational imposition fell on a ready audience despite the objections of some of the devoted progressives who remained oriented to the attitudes of the 1920s rather than to the problems of the 1930s. Curti stated in *The Social Ideas of American Educators* that many followed Counts in giving up their opposition to indoctrination of social attitudes. Foremost among those devoted to the child-centered movement in progressivism was the well-known popularizer of the "project method," William H. Kilpatrick. In his own work of social criticism, *Education and the Social Crisis* (1932) Kilpatrick urged the casting away of aloofness of education from social problems and a more explicit orientation of organized education to social reconstruction.[29] It is of interest to note that while many of the progressives associated with public education supported Counts's views on imposition, many of those opposed had pioneered in the early private progressive experimental schools. Although Counts's general message of building a new social order seemed to voice the unspoken words of many educators, it was his bold urging of educational imposition which severed the ties to the past. This won him a place of significance in the annals of the history of American education.

Throughout his writings, Counts urged educators to abandon what he called the naïve faith that the school was a neutral institution. Education, he reiterated, could serve any cause —tyranny as well as freedom, ignorance as well as enlightenment. Whether education was good or evil depended not on the laws of learning but on the conception of life and of civilization which gave it substance and direction. If education was to advance the cause of human freedom, it had to be explicitly designed for that purpose.[30]

In retrospect, the controversy over committed education focused on the concept of "open-mindedness." Both schools of progressive educators, those who accepted imposition and those who rejected it, claimed to be influenced by John Dewey's instrumentalist philosophy. In *The Quest for Certainty* (1929) Dewey advocated the supremacy of the scientific method and argued against the dualisms which occurred when alleged a priori truths and antecedent realities entered the areas of knowledge and action. In *Democracy and Education*, Dewey concluded that life was development and that developing or growing was life. Dewey stated that "the educational process has no end beyond itself; it is its own end; and that the educational process is one of continuing reorganizing, reconstructing, transforming." [31]

Since, according to Dewey, the end of education was growth for the sake of further growth, was Counts's suggested imposition of democratic collectivism a violation of open-mindedness and the criteria of growth? Moreover, since truth was not fixed and final but rather a warranted assertability according to the scientific method of instrumentalism, was not the imposition of democratic collectivism a violation of the instrumentalist method? Some critics such as Milton C. Cummings charged that Counts violated the experimental method. In urging the rejection of Counts's imposition, Cummings advocated an education based on a method of thought rather than on a set of predetermined goals. This experimentalist opponent of imposition said:

It is most highly challenging to critical thought and considered action because no absolutes are admitted, and the
consequences of each plan on human life are kept at the
very focus of attention. Conclusions are not buckled in a
strait-jacket for all time to come, but the process of thinking itself makes for high conviction and courageous
determination because there is supporting evidence.[32]

John Childs stated that Counts fully agreed with Dewey's
view that the concept of democracy was foundational in determining the ends and means of American education. Democracy signified the moral effort to organize social life on
the basis of respect for the dignity and worth of each member
of society. According to Childs, both Dewey and Counts agreed
that the goal of all intellectual and social effort was to provide
the concrete life conditions which released the capacities of
human beings from whatever curbed and repressed them.[33]
Childs further concluded that Counts shared the major pragmatic concepts developed by Dewey which sought the development of a philosophy in harmony with evolutionary principles,
attitudes and methods of experimental inquiry, and the values
of democracy.[34]

At this point it might be remarked that both Counts and
Dewey, one who favored and one who opposed imposition,
agreed that democracy should serve as the end of education.
Perhaps a word of clarification might serve to illustrate how
their positions were similar and how they differed. For Dewey,
the sole end of education was growth for the sake of further
growth. This end, growth, had no fixed or predetermined end
outside of the death of the organism. Rather it served to develop the potentialities of each individual person through active experience based upon the resolution of life problems. Us-

ing the scientific method as the methodology for solving problems, the best environment which allowed for the free play of critical intelligence or reflective thinking was that of a democratic society. Thus, democracy became synonymous with growth or at least synonymous with the environment which allowed the necessary conditions for the fullest degree of growth.

To the progressive who opposed imposition, Dewey's concept of growth was a satisfactory educational end. To these persons, however, anything that blocked the free development of the child inhibited growth. Allegiance to any fixed social or political creed constituted a predetermined end which blocked growth. Thus, the progressives who stressed educational neutrality did so out of a concern for their conception of democracy and the free play of intelligence associated with that concept of democracy.

Like Dewey, and like the neutralist progressives, Counts, too, believed in democracy as the sole end of education. However, for him, at least during the 1930s, this was a special concept of democracy. Since the tendency to growth could be blocked by social, political, and economic barriers to the development of the human potentiality, economic depression and the dominance of an economic aristocracy were obstacles to growth. These had to be eliminated from a truly democratic society. As revealed in *The Social Foundations of Education* (1934) and *The Prospects of American Democracy* (1938), Counts fashioned a special meaning for his conception of democracy which he termed democratic collectivism. Faithful to the conception of the open-endedness of the scientific method, or lacking a clear-cut formulation of his own meaning of democratic collectivism, this concept remained vague and clouded to many of his listeners, even to his admirers. As Henry Holmes inquired in his article, "The Teacher in Politics," just exactly what did Counts want teachers to do on the concrete and immediate levels in the school? Two answers emerge as to why Counts did not elaborate a specific program: one, the contours of the educational program, like that of the social program, were to be fashioned by the creative intelligence of the American people; or two, his message was that of an inspiring preachment for a great crusade to an ill-defined action.

In *Social Frontier*, John Dewey allied himself with the program of building a new social order. Although he did not think that the schools in any literal sense could build such an order, he believed that the schools could share in the process as they allied themselves with this or that movement of the existing social forces in America. In the past the schools, according to Dewey, furthered the contemporary social drift by promoting an economic form of success which was intrinsically pecuniary and egoistic. By accommodation to the existing conditions, the teachers had committed themselves to the old and chaotic. As the teachers of the nation had once committed themselves to the old order of economic individualism, they could also transfer their allegiance to the emergent collectivistic society:

> If he or she is genuinely committed to allegiance with present forces that tend to develop a social order which will, through collective control and ownership, make possible a genuine and needed "rugged individualism" (in the sense of individuality) for all members of the community, the teachers will, moreover, not be content with generalities about the desired future order.[35]

Dewey, further, outlined the task of education to translate the desired ideal into concrete detail in administration, instruction, and subject matter. Unless this determined effort was made, Dewey feared that choice would be made unconsciously by yielding to exigencies of immediate pressures and of estimating success in terms of egoistic ambitions.[36]

It would seem that both Dewey and Counts were not widely separated on the view that the school could share in building the new social order. Both agreed that the nature of this social order would be collectivistic. The area where possible difference might arise was in the realm of educational method. Both expressed devotion to the free method of scientific inquiry. The question remained could the free inquiry of science proceed in the light of a prior commitment to democratic collectivism such as that urged by Counts?

Writing in 1969, Counts reiterated the views that he had expressed on indoctrination almost forty years earlier. He reasserted his belief that indoctrination was an inevitable and inescapable aspect of educating the young in any society. The human child, he said, was born helpless but possessed infinite potentialities for growth in all directions. Although every human being was unique as an individual, he was still molded by the context of that culture in which he lived. Education, both informally and formally, involved the total process of inducting the young into the culture with " its ways of acting, feeling, thinking, its language, its tools, its institutions, its ethical and aesthetic values, its basic ideas, religious doctrines, and philosophical presuppositions." [37] Although the culture was imposed upon the child in every educational situation, Counts firmly rejected the proposition that anything should be taught as absolutely fixed and final. In a democratic society, disciplined criticism was especially needed. The critically minded person was the product of an education that carefully cultivated the intellectual virtues of accuracy, precision, truthfulness, openmindedness, and integrity.[38]

Before discussing the issue of educational methodology,

Counts's proposals for improving the curriculum and teacher education will be examined. These vital areas had a profound and essential influence on the question of instructional methodology.

1. George S. Counts, *The American Road to Culture* (New York: John Day Co., 1930), pp. 32–33.

2. Ibid., pp. 186–87.

3. "Introductory Remarks on Indoctrination," *Social Frontier,* 1 (1935), 8.

4. Ibid., p. 9.

5. Counts, *The Social Foundations of Education* (New York: Charles Scribner's Sons, 1934), p. 536.

6. Counts, *The Prospects of American Democracy* (New York: John Day Co., 1938), p. 317.

7. Counts, "Education for What?" Part I, *New Republic,* 71 (May 18, 1932), 14.

8. Counts, *Dare the Schools Build a New Social Order?* (New York: John Day Co., 1932), p. 13.

9. Counts, "Theses on Freedom, Culture, and Social Planning and Leadership," *National Education Association Proceedings,* 70 (1932), 249.

10. Ibid.

11. Counts, *Social Foundations,* p. 253.

12. Counts, "Theses," p. 249.

13. Ibid.

14. Counts, *Dare the Schools,* pp. 15–16.

15. Counts, "Education For What?" Part I, p. 14.

16. Counts, "Dare Progressive Education Be Progressive?" *Progressive Education,* 9 (1932), 259.

17. Counts, *Dare the Schools,* p. 16.

18. Counts, *Social Foundations,* pp. 537–38.

19. Counts, *Dare the Schools*, p. 11.

20. Counts, *Soviet Challenge to America* (New York: John Day Co., 1931), p. 317.

21. Counts, *Dare the Schools*, p. 17.

22. "The Position of the Social Frontier," *Social Frontier*, 1 (1935), 30.

23. Counts, *Dare the Schools*, p. 20.

24. Elsie R. Clapp, "Learning and Indoctrinating," *Progressive Education*, 9 (1932), 270.

25. Ellen Geer, "The Courage to Keep an Open Mind," *Progressive Education*, 9 (1932), 267.

26. Henry W. Holmes, "The Teacher in Politics," *Progressive Education*, 9 (1932), 414.

27. Ibid., pp. 415–16.

28. Counts, *Social Foundations*, p. 537.

29. Merle Curti, *The Social Ideas of American Educators* (Paterson, N.J.: Littlefield, Adams & Co., 1959), pp. 574–75.

30. Counts, *Education and the Foundations of Human Freedom* (Pittsburgh: University of Pittsburgh Press, 1962), p. 54.

31. John Dewey, *Democracy and Education* (New York: Macmillan Co., 1916), p. 59.

32. Milton C. Cummings, "How Can the Schools Build a New Social Order?" *School and Society*, 36 (1932), 757.

33. John L. Childs, *American Pragmatism and Education* (New York: Henry Holt & Co., 1956), p. 219.

34. Ibid., pp. 216–17.

35. John Dewey, "Can Education Share in Social Reconstruction?" *Social Frontier*, 1 (1934), 12.

36. Ibid.

37. Counts, "Should the Teacher Always Be Neutral?" *Phi Delta Kappan*, LI (1969), 187.

38. Ibid., 188.

VI. The Curriculum

Counts's educational philosophy and program designed to facilitate transition to the emergent age of democratic collectivism necessarily involved consideration of the school's curriculum. In the light of the problems of cultural transition and economic dislocation, he analyzed the curriculum of the American public school. In doing so, he focused attention on the tremendous growth of the curriculum in the industrial era, the need for a cooperative program of curriculum construction, an emphasis of a social orientation in subject matter, and the methodology of instruction. The secondary curriculum was an area of special interest for Counts. Since the time of his *The Senior High School Curriculum* (1926), he had studied the program and philosophy of the public school curriculum. During the 1930s, he served as research director of the Commission of the American Historical Association on the Social Studies in the Schools. In *The Social Foundations of Education* (1934), he analyzed the social studies curriculum. Since the curriculum contained both the means and ends of the public education program,

Counts's suggested curriculum must be considered in view of his educational philosophy and program.

Curriculum Expansion

As stated earlier, Counts attributed curriculum expansion to the increased complexity of an industrialized and technological society. Conditioned by business and industrial needs, concentration on classics and mathematics gradually declined while that of modern languages, natural science, history, social sciences, technology, and the arts increased. In addition to the proliferation of subject matter specialties, innumerable extracurricular activities entered the school program. The expanded curriculum developed after 1900 resulted from the efforts of organized education to meet the diverse needs of the expanded school population.[1]

Although the nation was experiencing cultural transition during the very period of curriculum expansion, Counts found that educators made no deliberate effort to guide the developing curriculum towards the social needs of a technological society. Since the turn of the century, the public high school, in particular, was in a state of transition with the curriculum in flux. Although the older faith in faculty discipline diminished, Counts asserted that no clearly formulated educational theory had replaced it.[2] It was commonly assumed that the school should offer any program of study believed to lead to individual success. In curriculum construction, the school responded to various interior and exterior pressures. Since the school lacked an integrating educational philosophy, Counts charged that educational authorities shifted the burden of responsibility and choice to pupils and parents. Influenced by methods of business efficiency, the school resembled a machine which distributed certificates and degrees to the rising generation.[3]

In criticizing this haphazard curriculum expansion, Counts charged that educators had neglected critical study of social life and institutions. The curriculum was conservative and rested on a traditional rather than scientific basis. The most striking tendency in curriculum expansion, he asserted, was that of adding rather than deleting obsolete courses. Within the school, vested interests supporting an established course or practice were stronger than those proposing innovation. Greater opposition occurred against dropping an old subject than against introducing a new one. Since no rational or general approach developed, an unintegrated, unwieldly high school curriculum resulted.[4]

With this educational confusion generated by the ignoring of cultural demands and by the desire of self-perpetuation by vested educational interests, the curriculum became isolated and remote from life. As earlier indicated, in industrial society the school assumed functions previously administered by other educational institutions such as home and community. In industrial society, Counts alleged, the separation of the industry from the home produced an education which lacked meaning for many youngsters. As a result, the curriculum became bookish and unreal.

Counts found this confused situation complicated still further by the pluralistic character of American society. The modern urban center, composed of numerous conflicting groups and organizations, lacked unity of interest and ideals. Divided into various political parties, religious sects, economic classes, and special interest groups, conflicting economic, political, religious, and moral attitudes characterized American society. Each of these groups promoted special interests by seeking to incorporate its own peculiar view into the public school curriculum. The school, Counts stated, then became a convenient propaganda instrument. If the school was to perform a rationally determined social function, the curriculum planning should be placed in the hands of professionally trained experts. Without expert planning and organization, Counts warned, the curriculum was destined to serve as a battleground of vested subject specialists within and conflicting pressure groups without.[5]

Before specifically considering the task of curriculum-making, Counts contrasted two different approaches to the problem of the curriculum. In *The American Road to Culture* (1930) he stated that a fundamental and irreconcilable difference of opinion existed among educational theorists on the problem of curriculum. On the one hand, some theorists held that the function of the school was essentially conservative. In contrast, others conceived the school as an agency of social reconstruction. Although the conservatives retarded, they did not prevent the entry of new subjects into the curriculum. Counts stated, rapid curriculum changes attested to the operation of social forces in society. Nevertheless under the direction of the conservative curriculum-makers, agencies outside of the school such as local chambers of commerce, labor unions, and religious groups influenced the shaping of the public school program. The conservative curriculum-maker was primarily concerned with arangement and organization of instructional materials used in the school. Many of these theorists, associated with the scientific movement in education, insisted that the foremost problem in curriculum construction was methodological. Counts charged that the conservative ignored social analysis.[6]

According to Counts, the more culturally oriented, social

reconstructionist theorist believed that the curriculum should be based on analysis of the emergent tendencies in civilization. They subjected institutions and practices to scrutiny in order to fashion a curriculum which originated with the educational profession and responded to social needs. In disagreeing with the conservative, the reconstructionist, according to Counts, held that no amount of purely objective study of life activities produced standards which distinguished good from bad. Unfortunately, Counts observed, the social reconstructionists lacked a practical proposal of ways and means of converting the school into a great creative social force.[7] After contrasting these two widely variant views, Counts stated that the crucial point in curriculum-making was in the selection of judges. Obviously, the school program reflected the attitudes and values of those who selected materials, purposes, and aims of the educational program. Counts therefore directed attention to the selection of the curriculum-maker.

Selection of the Curriculum-Maker

According to Counts, the task of curriculum construction was complex, difficult, and unsuited to the amateur. Not to be left to the decisions of any single individual, curriculum construction was a cooperative venture on the part of those expertly trained in educational problems. With this view, Counts discussed who should and who should not make the curriculum.

Counts stated that the curriculum construction should not devolve on unqualified persons regardless of the importance of their role in community and society. Among those cited as unqualified for the task, Counts singled out state legislatures, boards of education, powerful minority groups, colleges, and vested subject matter specialists. Although these groups had exercised great influence in the building of the curriculum in the past, they were unsuited for the task.

State legislatures, Counts said, were increasingly interested in the curriculum. Laws such as that prohibiting the teaching of evolution, as in Tennessee, revealed the temper and incompetence of the legislatures. The average legislator lacked the professional educational training and experience needed for curriculum construction. Counts stated, however, that this deficiency did not deter certain legislators from seeking to express themselves through the curriculum. Like the state legislatures, board of education members were also unqualified. The responsibility of the board of education was to state general educational policy. Even in this function, they revealed undesirable bias on behalf of the privileged.[8]

As stated, Counts found that the industrialized, urban community contained many highly organized and articulate groups. On the basis of their own special interests, these organizations attempted to modify the curriculum. Frequently devoted to special interests, these groups often were unconcerned about the general welfare and were unsuited to deal with the problems of curriculum construction.[9]

Counts singled out two educational groups which were not to be entrusted with the task of curriculum construction, the colleges and subject matter specialists. Colleges had historically been one of the most potent forces in shaping the secondary school curriculum. Although the control by the college of the high school had weakened, the struggle for institutional freedom continued as the college attempted to restrict the high school curriculum to traditional subject matter areas. In addition to the influence of the college, Counts found the secondary school hampered in efforts to reconstruct their programs by the departmentalization of work within the high school and the emphasis on narrowly training the high school teacher in subject matter specialization. Counts observed that the protective behavior of special vested interest groups negated much of the work involved in curriculum-making. Instead of teachers who were subject matter specialists, Counts stated the high school needed teachers who were experts in secondary education.[10]

In his study of the high school curriculum, Counts wrote that the construction of an adequate curriculum required cooperative efforts of at least seven types of persons: psychologist, sociologist, philosopher, specialist in selecting and organizing materials, classroom teacher, expert in curriculum appraisal, and the high school administrator. To Counts, the inclusion of the psychologist was obvious since at every level, education concerned the nature of the learner. An adequate secondary school curriculum reflected knowledge dealing with the learning attitudes, abilities, interests, and aptitudes.[11]

As stated many times, Counts's over-all educational philosophy rested on a civilizational foundation. Education introduced the immature to social life and the use of cultural institutions and instrumentalities. Since the educational program of the school transmitted the social heritage to the young, the sociologist, an expert in analyzing civilization, was indispensable in curriculum construction.[12] It is probable that Counts's inclusion of the sociologist also reflected his own interest in sociology.

Counts assigned a major role in curriculum construction to the philosopher who was to develop a coherent value scheme and formulate social and educational purposes. As soon as it became necessary to choose between alternative programs representing divergent life syles, the curriculum-maker faced an axiological problem. One of the greatest needs of organized education was a restatement of purposes originating from a complete synthesis of science, aesthetics, and ethics. This formulation could neglect no area of human experience.[13]

Counts included the classroom teacher as a member of the cooperative curriculum committee. The curriculum remained inert material until possessed and used by the teacher who had to cast the raw materials into the forms necessary to achieve the desired educational goals. For Counts, the teacher was more than a subject matter specialist; he was an artist in guiding the learning process and in developing the personality of the learner.[14]

After formulating educational purposes, it was necessary to turn to persons expert in selecting and organizing instructional materials. The theoretical findings of psychologists, sociologists, and philosophers required translation into the materials which could be tested by actual experimentation in the school. After the work of the expert in selection and organization, the cooperative curriculum group needed the advice of persons trained in curriculum appraisal. Ways and means of curriculum appraisal had to be devised in light of recent social trends. Counts found the technique for measuring the influence of the high school program, in particular, almost totally lacking.[15] Finally, the school administrator or high school principal organized, coordinated, and integrated the efforts of the different specialists. The administrator, too, had the difficult task of supplying the leadership in securing community assent to the reconstruction of curriculum.[16]

Counts's suggested cooperative method of curriculum formulation involved difficulty and complexity. Undoubtedly, the efforts of special interest groups, both internal and external to the school, could block realization of public interests. Interference by unqualified amateurs further confused the task. Counts's inclusion of the sociologist, philosopher, and psychologist in the cooperative group corresponded to his interdisciplinary conception of education.

The classroom teacher's presence in planning and building the curriculum fulfilled an obvious function. More than a subject matter specialist, the classroom teacher also was concerned with learning processes. In his works during the 1930s, Counts attacked pedagogues who emphasized teaching methods but ignored subject matter. However, his effort to limit subject matter specialization in the secondary school could have had the adverse effect of encouraging teachers to concentrate exclusively on methodology. Although the subject matter specialist who attempted to perpetuate his own subject as a vested interest was undesirable as a curriculum planner, knowledge of a particular subject was vital in constructing a curriculum which included that particular subject.

Counts also focused attention on the work of experts in selection and organization of the materials of instruction and the curriculum appraiser. Although he included these experts, he failed to clearly delineate their training and function. Once again, it seemed that the expert in selection and organization of materials needed some specialization in subject matter to guard against the tendency to develop a methodology divorced from subject matter to which Counts so strenuously objected.

Need For Curriculum Reconstruction

Counts's earlier survey of the rapid expansion of the curriculum since the turn of the century revealed glaring inadequacies in the school's program. Subjected to pressure groups, haphazard in development, and lacking an over-all purpose and a guiding philosophy, the curriculum needed critical study and reconstruction. For Counts, the curriculum embraced the entire life of the school as well as subjects of study. Before the details were filled in, the general curriculum plan should be outlined. Counts called for weighing of values and adjudication of conflict in the light of scientifically determined needs rather than on the basis of the relative power of vested interest groups.[17] Finding the contemporary curriculum organized primarily for administrative efficiency rather than for educational values, Counts urged that democratic social purposes permeate and unify the entire school program.[18] Although Counts recommended adjudication of conflicts, he failed to indicate a precise methodological formula for bringing about such adjudication or consensus.

For Counts, the primary objective of education was establishment of certain controls or dispositions which guided conduct. The effective curriculum had to be defined and organized in terms of desired behavioral changes. Unfortunately, Counts asserted, the American system of public education operated within the hierarchy of values associated with economic individualism which postulated profit-making through competition as the highest goal. The school instilled the ideal that the best philosophy of life was competitive. Counts had rejected the social and educational philosophy of economic individualism many times before.

Counts urged curriculum reconstruction according to the ideal of democratic collectivism. This would, he said, not require the addition of new subjects. The same subjects would be taught and the same activities organized. Children would learn to read, write, figure, work, and play together. However, the spirit, approach, and orientation would be different from that of the traditional curriculum. Appeals to egocentric and selfish impulses would be subordinated, and instead, emphasis placed on social, cooperative, and creative impulses. No individual would be rewarded for overcoming and surpassing another.[19]

The Social Science Curriculum

As research director of the Commission of the American Historical Association on the Social Studies in the Schools from 1931 to 1933, Counts devoted particular attention to the social science curriculum. In view of his civilizational philosophy of education, history and the social sciences constituted necessary areas of study.

In *The Social Foundations of Education* (1934) Counts stated that social science instruction should be based upon the maturation of the child and build upon, facilitate, and direct the maturation process. Beginning with the immediate and moving towards the remote, the child should be taken in the first year of elementary school and systematically led out of the family, neighborhood, and community into the state, nation, and world. The systematic exposure to the connections between the near and remote built a network of experience and created a general recognition of the interdependence of the modern world. As the method of instruction proceded from the near to the far, it also moved from the present into the past. The child, then, developed a sense of time and awareness of the cultural heritage as he studied customs, institutions, ideas, interests, and conflicts. As the child matured, the instructional emphasis shifted from surface to depth and from mere data and fact to thought. Although industrial civilization had isolated the school, much of this isolation could be overcome by reducing to the narrowest possible proportions the distance from life. He recommended the close integration of classroom instruction with social life and labor. From the most elementary to the most advanced levels, he urged a single process of social science instruction which carried the individual to wider and more intense understandings and appreciations.[20]

In basing arrangement of the materials of social science instruction upon the maturation of the child, Counts closely paralleled Dewey's second level of curriculum. Dewey stated that from infancy the child gradually pushed back the boundaries of his immediate world along the two dimensions of time and space and thus widened his knowledge and increased his powers of thought and action. By moving out from the immediate locality, the child entered the widening spatial realm of geography. By moving from the present into the past, the child entered the broadening realm of history. In *Democracy and Education* (1916) Dewey stressed the teaching of history and geography in what he termed the second level of curriculum. For him, geography and history were the two great school resources for enlarging the significance of direct personal experience. He stated that, "while history makes human implications explicit and geography natural connections, these subjects are two phases of the same living whole, since the life of men in association goes on in nature, not as an accidental setting, but as the material and medium of development." [21]

Like Counts, Dewey stressed history as the key to the present. Both Dewey and Counts found the aim of education to be the induction of the immature into the culture. In stressing the importance of the cultural heritage, both emphasized the role of history and geography and agreed that the past became significant in relation to the present. As Dewey said, "past events cannot be separated from the living present and retain meaning. The true starting point of history is always some present situation with its problems." [22]

Counts urged that the social studies curriculum be given a genuinely social meaning. For example, he urged the teaching of geography, not merely as a body of useful and interesting material, but as the physical basis for building a finer civilization and culture. Natural resources were to be regarded as the possessions of all the people and not as exploitive areas of profit-seeking and accumulation of private wealth. [23]

For Counts, the framework of the social sciences rested in the bedrock of democratic collectivism. As already indicated, he regarded American society as moving from a loosely organized to a closely integrated economy. Within American history, there existed a body of materials which furnished direction to the course of development of American institutions. Counts urged the selection and organization of materials in teaching of the social sciences on the basis of the needs of a society moving from individualism to a form of democratic collectivism conceived and administered in the interests of the popular masses. [24]

To develop the appropriate loyalties and attitudes for democratic collectivism, Counts suggested that the social sciences depict the lives and fortunes of the ordinary people. This historical portrayal of the collective life of the common man was to focus on the Western world and North America. For a society of equal men, emphasis on the life of the common people seemed more rational than the traditional stress placed on aristocrats, princes, kings, and emperors. [25] Emphasis on the historical struggles and achievements of the common people also promoted the building of values appropriate to a democratic society managed in the common interests.

Counts recommended that the social studies trace the evolution of peaceful arts and culture. He did not suggest that the school ignore the history of warfare since it was too tragic and central to be deleted from the record. The objective, however, was not to glorify war as heroic, but rather to provide understanding of war as a social phenomenon generating misery and suffering. Instead of glorifying conquering military heroes, the social studies were to emphasize the achievements of the creative figures of the past such as inventors, explorers, organizers, statesmen, teachers, scientists, artists, and philosophers. Above all, Counts urged, it should be stressed that human culture was not produced by any single nation but rather was the common achievement of many races and peoples working together and striving throughout history.[26] In the building of a value schema for the age of collectivism, Counts first had to dethrone the old heroes. In their stead, new heroes, worthy of emulation, were erected as exemplars for the rising generation.

Since democracy was crucial in the American cultural heritage, Counts recommended that the social studies curriculum outline the ideal of democracy in such a way as to capture the imagination of youth and give the American educational program an abiding goal. He urged that democracy be identified with the worth and dignity of the common man. On the basis of democracy's egalitarian origins, the student would then be led to a study of certain of the great religious and humanistic movements.[27]

A second major element in Counts's theory of American society was the rise of industrial and technological society. Along with the democratic heritage, the social science curriculum was to retell the growth of industrial civilization and

the emergence of an integrated economy. The development of
science and technology and the growth of man's control over
nature would be brought into focus. The cultural repercus-
sions of the new forces in all areas of life would be studied.
Social studies instruction would examine the passing of laissez
faire, the reunion of economics and politics, the rise of social
planning, and the movement toward world integration and
organization.[28]

After carefully studying the evolution and importance of
democracy and industrial society in American civilization, social science instruction was to describe the numerous social
conflicts. Counts urged that contradictions such as prosperity
and poverty, privations and riches, starvation in the midst of
plenty, invention converted into instruments of debasing society, and the corruption of government by vested interests be
studied as a part of social science instruction. Students were
not to be deflected from unpleasant social realities; rather they
were to study, examine, and seek to resolve these social problems. Counts warned that the transmission of the democratic
ideal to students without providing for criticism of contemporary institutional arrangements and practices was hypocritical.
If the school was to function as an instrument of purification,
it had to systematically expose contemporary social evils. It
should not convey the false impression that the democratic
ideal had been fulfilled in the United States.[29]

Counts's listing of conflict areas indicated his value commitment to democratic collectivism. These conflicts had been
produced by the prevailing system of economic individualism.
The resolution of social conflict inevitably involved the con-
demnation of the forces which produced them.

As an instrument of social improvement, the school would
constantly investigate social, political, and economic proposals,

programs, and philosophies. Among the philosophies to be examined, Counts listed capitalism, syndicalism, anarchism, socialism, distributism, communism, and fascism. He urged examination not only of their theoretical implications, but also of the practical results wherever these theories were practiced. Each proposal, regardless of origin, was to undergo critical examination in the light of American history and democracy. The contemporary problems of cultural transition and economic dislocation demanded that informed intelligence be distributed throughout the population.[30] It will be recalled that Counts proposed a program of political action designed to cope with the problems of economic depression and the growth of economic aristocracy. His proposed critical examination of competing political ideologies was designed to further the political sensibilities of the American public. This examination was not to be purely objective but rather was to take place against the yardstick of democratic values.

In his discussion of the social studies curriculum, Counts postulated a program to further the advance of democratic collectivism among the purposes of the school. The selection of areas of study closely corresponded with his analysis of American society. Democracy and technology emerged as primary units of study. His selection of areas to study also coincided with his demands for a committed educational program. In his recommendation that areas of conflict and competing philosophies be studied, Counts departed from the traditional view of the teaching of the social studies. In advocating that communism and fascism be examined critically, he differed from many conservative educators and certain noneducational groups which demanded that history and social studies promote nationalistic patriotism.

Other Areas in the Curriculum

Sharing in experimentalism and regarding science as a crucial component in the technological order, Counts urged exploration of the social role of science and technology. In *The Principles of Education* (1924) he recommended cultivation of the scientific temper and critical evaluation of every social invention on the basis of available evidence. An effort must be made, he said, to cultivate an open-mindedness eager for continuous inquiry holding all conclusions tentatively, and forever youthful and hopeful.[31] Science and technology were not leisure time activities, nor instruments of a special class devoted to personal aggrandizement. Rather science and technology were man's most valuable instruments in his long struggle with environment.[32] Given a social orientation, they were not mechanical methods but rather were humanistic forces for man's continued material and spiritual betterment.

Art was not to be taught primarily as a vehicle of individual expression but rather as a means of enriching and beautifying common life. Once again Counts paralleled Dewey's views. In *Art as Experience,* Dewey argued against exiling art to a separate realm where it was isolated from the materials and aims of human action and achievements.[33] Like Dewey, Counts stated that art should not be relegated to museums and art galleries but rather used and taught to bring beauty of line, form, and color to factories, cities, highways, parks, public buildings, and objects of ordinary use and dwellings.[34]

Counts's view of the curriculum also provided for specialized training. He commented that a society based on a collective economy required proficiency in the entire occupational range. Vocational training should never be narrow but always contain social purposes. The program of occupational preparedness should be organized on the basis of social needs rather than in terms of the ambitions of particular institutions, departments, or persons. Care should also be exercised lest the specialist regard his training as private property for exploiting the weak and unfortunate at public expense. Counts urged a determined effort to coordinate training facilities in harmony with economic needs.[35]

Although stressing social utility, the curriculum envisioned by Counts was not narrowly utilitarian. Educational emphasis, he said, depended on the richness of natural resources, level of technology, and pressure of population on the means of subsistence. With the removal of competition and conspicuous consumption of goods and services, he believed it possible to release energies for cultural and spiritual growth and eventually subordinate economic concerns.[36]

Despite the emphasis on cooperative activities, Counts still recommended high individual achievement. To him, democratic collectivism did not mean imposition of a single standard of mediocrity. Rather in a closely integrated society, the fullest development of the varied gifts and abilities in the population was demanded by the general welfare. To overlook personal talent in any field of social usefulness or cultural worth involved not only injustice, but also wasted valuable natural resources. All were to contribute to raising the material and cultural level of the entire population. The curriculum of the public school was to be devoted to that end.[37]

Method of Thought

In his discussion of the curriculum, Counts revealed more concern with content than with process or method. According to Childs, Counts believed emphasis on methodology constituted escape from the responsibilities of indicating the reconstructive course of the educational program.[38] In *The Principles of Education,* Counts defined education as a social process which was an economical method of assisting an initially illadapted individual, during the short span of a single life, to cope with the ever increasing complexities of the world.[39] Like Dewey, Counts believed that learning occurred as the individual confronted problematic situations within his experience. Counts stated that thought was occasioned by some problem which necessitated adaptation on the part of the individual through a process of trial and error in the mental rather than in the motor realm. Only when a situation occurred in which past experience provided no ready-made mode of behavior was the reflective, or problem-solving process necessary.[40]

Counts accepted Dewey's formulation of the method of reflective experience or problem-solving based on the scientific method. This method consisted of the well-known five steps: one, perplexity, confusion, doubt arising from implication in an undetermined and incomplete situation; two, a tentative interpretation of the situation and a view of the consequences which might follow certain actions; three, examination, inspection, exploration, and analysis of the problematic situation to define and clarify; four, elaboration of tentative hypotheses of action; and five, the testing of the hypothesis acted upon.[41]

The Principles of Education (1924) by Counts and J. Crosby Chapman, used an educational approach which was very similar to that of John Dewey. This early work accepted habit psychology and problem-solving as the basis of thought.[42] Although always holding the problem-solving approach in high esteem, Counts by the 1930s believed that problem-solving of itself as a sole educational method was inadequate. At the 1932 meeting of the National Education Association, he stated that he agreed with Herman H. Horne that problem-solving was inadequate as a sole educational approach. He further stated that American education had developed a theory of learning which involved more than the problem-solving approach.[43]

Once again relying on the interpretation of John Childs, the limitations which Counts placed on the problem-solving method can be readily seen. Undoubtedly, these limitations also were directed to the project method of William H. Kilpatrick and others. Childs stated that Counts believed that what to think was intimately connected with how to think. The mastery of conclusions in a given field was a necessary prerequisite for significant inquiry into that particular subject. To master the conclusions, the student first had to master the facts and principles of interpretation involved in them. Thinking took place only with reference to a particular context.[44]

According to Childs, Counts believed that the project method and activities were worthwhile in the early years of education. As the student advanced to the higher educational levels, the body of materials studied became differentiated. Although this differentiation pointed to a subject matter approach, teachers were to be prepared to go beyond subject matter specialization to an examination of the civilization which the school served.[45]

Childs stated that Counts did not believe that the traditional school projects such as dress-making, cooking, or gardening provided sufficient scope for the richest development of the young. Instead Counts viewed the method of historical and social analysis, the study of the past and an orientation to present problems, as a more important mode of problem-solving. Thus the present situation was blended with the past into a common act of thought.[46]

Thus in discussion of a methodology of learning, Counts advocated understanding of the existent bodies of knowledge. By understanding the achievements in certain areas of knowledge, students would know how to locate their problems and use the past experience of the race in solving present problems. He did not recommend relying solely on the project method. Rather problem solving and the project method were fused with the systematic study of organized subject areas. It should be pointed out in this brief discussion of the educational method advocated by Counts that he spoke only rarely on methodology and confined himself primarily to social analysis of education.

Before summarizing the educational theory of Counts by means of an examination of his educational proposals, some word should be mentioned concerning his proposals for teacher education. Since he trusted in the teachers to aid in the building of a new social order, the following chapter will discuss teacher education in the United States.

1. George S. Counts, *The Social Foundations of Education* (New York: Charles Scribner's Sons, 1934), p. 271.

2. Counts, *The Senior High School Curriculum* (Chicago: University of Chicago Press, 1926), p. 145.

3. Counts, *Social Foundations,* p. 271.

4. Counts, "Who Shall Make the Curriculum?" *School Review,* 35 (1927), 333.

5. Counts, *Senior High School*, p. 128.

6. Counts, *The American Road to Culture* (New York: John Day Co., 1930), p. 124.

7. Ibid., p. 126.

8. Counts, "Who Shall Make?", 334–35.

9. Ibid., 336.

10. Ibid., 336–37.

11. Ibid., 337.

12. Ibid.

13. Ibid., 337–38.

14. Ibid., 338.

15. Ibid.

16. Ibid., 339.

17. Counts, *Senior High School*, p. 149.

18. Counts, *Social Foundations*, p. 544.

19. Ibid.

20. Ibid., p. 554.

21. John Dewey, *Democracy and Education* (New York: Macmillan Co., 1916), p. 255.

22. Ibid., p. 251.

23. Counts, *Social Foundations*, p. 546.

24. Ibid., p. 549.

25. Ibid.

26. Ibid., p. 550.

27. Ibid., pp. 550–51.

28. Ibid., p. 551.

29. Ibid., p. 551–52.

30. Ibid., p. 553.

31. Chapman and Counts, *Principles of Education* (Chicago: Houghton Mifflin Co., 1924), p. 287.

32. Counts, *Social Foundations*, p. 546.

33. John Dewey, *Art as Experience* (1934; reprint ed., New York: G. P. Putnam's Sons, 1958), p. 1.

34. Counts, *Social Foundations,* p. 546.

35. Ibid., p. 547.

36. Ibid., pp. 545–46.

37. Ibid., p. 545.

38. John L. Childs, *American Pragmatism and Education* (New York: Henry Holt & Co., 1956), p. 222.

39. Chapman and Counts, *Principles,* p. 11.

40. Ibid., pp. 102–3.

41. Dewey, *Democracy,* p. 176.

42. Chapman and Counts, *Principles,* p. 72.

43. Counts, "Theses on Freedom, Culture, Social Planning, and Leadership," *National Education Association Proceedings,* 70 (1932), 252.

44. Childs, *American Pragmatism,* p. 224.

45. Ibid., p. 224.

46. Ibid., p. 246.

VII. Teacher Education

Counts's proposed program of education required teachers who were highly trained in social and cultural analysis. To ascertain the qualifications and preparation of teachers for such tasks, he examined patterns of teacher preparation in the United States. Counts critically analyzed the tradition which persisted well into modern times that held unnecessary an extended period of teacher education. This tradition originated with the pioneering life and methods used to establish and administer education on the frontier.[1] Schools were then organized by unlettered farmers. Until recently, Counts asserted that immature and poorly trained teachers staffed public schools. He found this tradition an encumbrance to developing an education for the technological age.

Inadequacy of Teacher Education

With the growth of American public education, training schools developed for teachers. American elementary teachers received preparation in normal schools and secondary teachers in colleges and universities. As teacher demand increased, schools of teacher training, too, increased. Despite the numerical increase, Counts asserted that these institutions offered an extremely narrow preparation. Stemming from a misconception of the nature of education and the role of the school, this narrow educational pattern emphasized pedagogic techniques and methods rather than a broad cultural view of education and society.

Counts stated that although schools and departments of education devoted exclusive energy to teacher preparation and the work of the school, their conception of education was astonishingly narrow. By ignoring other powerful social institutions, these schools cultivated only a fraction of their legitimate field. First, the schools and colleges of education accepted the naïve American notion that the school constituted the sole educative social institution. Counts had repeatedly stated that the school was only one of many educational social institutions. As a result of this misconception, duplication and conflict of function occurred among various educational agencies. These wasted energies perpetuated a partial conception of education. Although attempts at exploration of the cultural and social foundations of education occurred, Counts saw little hope for educational clarification until the many diverse educational agencies became conscious of each other and united in some form of institutional federation.[2] He further urged teacher education institutions to recognize this institutional relationship.

Secondly, Counts attacked the methodological preoccupation of many teacher training institutions. Overemphasis on methodology separated method from content. He found two groups of individuals guilty of causing this separation: professional educators and subject matter scholars. Further confusion resulted as each accused the other of encouraging inadequate teacher preparation.

Counts stated that many normal schools and teachers colleges conceived the teaching task as chiefly a methodological problem evolved independently of culture. They stressed teaching techniques and the "Science of Education." This emphasis resulted in narrowed interests and absorption in mechanics rather than the substance of teaching. Counts charged that the "Science of Education" assumed that an objective study of the processes of learning would result in the discovery of certain procedures which were independent and superior to culture. The "Science of Education" has already been discussed in the section dealing with educational responses during the 1930s. In attacking methodology divorced from content, he alleged that a methodology revolving around its own center was a form of sterile sophistry.[3]

Although concentration on an objective "Science of Education" had contributed to methodological pre-eminence, the growth of teacher training as a vested interest contributed still further to the ascendancy of the methodologist in teacher training. Once established, Counts observed, the normal school declared its independence and extended its jurisdiction. In emulation of other institutions, it established positions, salaries, emoluments, honors, titles, and privileges for distribution to methodologists. As teacher demand increased, many professional educators came to believe thorough subject matter preparation impossible. Counts charged that the normal schools specialized in techniques which poorly educated teachers repeated without difficulty. Thus method assumed the form of a cult and subjected teacher training to the tyranny of a pedagogical instrument.[4]

With their kingdom established, Counts charged that the methodologists gained increasing power over teacher preparation and the schools as they fortified their growing vested interests. Bringing pressure to bear upon state legislatures and state and local boards of education, methodologists secured adoption of laws requiring applicants for elementary and secondary teaching positions to present credentials attesting to completion of a specified number of courses in "education." According to Counts, no matter how competent in subject matter, the applicant could not obtain a teaching certificate without the prescribed number of pedagogical courses. Within the area of professional education, schools and professors emphasizing methodology received preferential treatment for proficiency in an area that Counts believed was loosely defined in both theory and practice.[5] Counts's attacks on educational methodology may seem unusual for a professor of education. These attacks were not directed to the discipline of education per se but rather to those who by their narrow approach monopolized the field. Like others concerned with the cultural implications of education, Counts advocated a program of teacher education rich in theoretical and social implications. The social, historical, and philosophical dimensions of education suffered from a narrow emphasis on methodology.

Counts did not confine his criticism of the narrow conception of teacher education solely to educational methodologists. He also criticized university professors who unconsciously aided the separation of method and content. Part of the responsibility for the separation of method and content and for the very establishment of separate teacher training institutions derived from trends within American higher learning. Concentrating exclusively on specialized research areas, many univer-

sity professors ignored teacher education. Counts charged
that many university professors scorned such "elementary" but
profoundly important problems as the instruction of the rising
generation and refused to consider the vital question of the relation of their specialties to the schools. Like the methodologists, they also protected vested interests. When brought into
connection with life, the sterility of much of this specialization
was exposed.[6] He further criticized the university's emphasis
on specialization to the detriment of general education. When
the university department engaged in teacher education, it
usually insisted on the introduction of the peculiar academic
mentality into the secondary and even elementary school.
Thus, Counts found prospective teachers restricted to two
wholly inadequate types of training. While one prepared for
action without understanding, the other prepared for understanding matters which had little relation to any probable
course of action.[7]

Need for a Culturally Oriented Teacher Education

After considering the inadequacies of the existent form of
teacher education, Counts suggested a culturally broadened
program. As stated, a narrow conception of teacher education
divorced the study of education from genuine social problems.
Many educators ignored the social implications of cultural
transition and economic depression. Indeed, Counts asserted
that the stereotyped curriculum of teacher education concentrated too much on buildings, equipment, finance, quantitative
measurements, and administrative arrangements and far too
little on the major social and educational problems of contem-

porary society.[8] To meet the pressing needs of American society, he called for "educational statesmanship" and a new program of teacher education.

In *The Social Foundations of Education,* Counts termed education one of the highest forms of statesmanship. As a public servant, the educator was obligated to foster the greatest possible development of the capacities of citizens upon which the state depended for existence, security, and fulfillment. The statesman-like educator would provide leadership for the nation and assume responsibilities for formulating educational philosophies, policies, and programs. This responsibility involved choice based upon dominant and emergent ethical and aesthetic values conceived in the light of the natural endowments, technological resources, cultural heritage, and great social trends.[9] Since the educational program rose no higher than the physical, intellectual, aesthetic, and moral qualifications of teachers, Counts urged the broadest possible teacher education. In the United States, the rapid expansion of the school and its assumption of major social responsibilities made organized education a significant force in shaping the national destiny.[10]

Intimately related to the call to statesmanship was the need for a new teacher education institution which would be a center of liberal learning and scholarship centering on the problems of an industrialized, democratic society. Thoroughly trained in his specialty, the prospective teacher should also study the history of American civilization, contemporary social trends, and his specialty's relationships to society.[11] Warning that this study must not assume a purely academic character, Counts stated that questions of national policy were not merely academic but rather instrumental in shaping educational programs. He urged the minimization of the purely technical aspects of teacher preparation and advocated a broad cultural program: "Education itself should be recognized, not as an independent and universal technique, but as an inseparable aspect of a particular culture in evolution. If education is ever divorced from this broad social process, it becomes formal and sterile." [12]

Cultural Foundations of Education

During the depression period, socially oriented, progressive educators realized that education needed to enter the arena of social controversy. Counts had early stressed this need in his civilizational or cultural philosophy of education. During the 1930s, other like-minded educators joined a discussion group at Teachers College of Columbia University to discuss informally the need of elaborating the cultural foundations of education. Among these progressive, socially oriented educators were Professors Kilpatrick, Rugg, Childs, Raup, Watson, Newlon and Brunner of Teachers College. John Dewey frequently attended the meetings, and Counts was a regular participant.[13] From this group derived the journal *Social Frontier*, edited by Counts, which advocated a policy of social reconstruction. Although an investigation of the meetings of this group lies beyond the scope of this study, this mention illustrates that Counts was not alone in advocating increased attention to the cultural foundations of education. He was rather a significant member of a community of opinion which characterized the progressive professors at Teachers College. This is not to say that complete accord existed within this community but rather a similar climate of opinion. Outside of this community, the more traditionally oriented educators such as

Isaac L. Kandel vigorously challenged the reconstructive tendencies of the group. Although the Dean of Teachers College, William F. Russell was tolerant of the group, he did not support their conclusions.[14] The chief importance of the conclusions of this discussion group was their agreement on a broadened program of teacher education. They agreed that the fields of the history of education, philosophy of education, comparative education, educational psychology, educational economics, and educational sociology had one primary purpose: to provide a firm foundation on which the technical specialty might rest. This recognition paved the way for the eventual consolidation of these formerly separate fields into a single division in 1934.[15] This reorganization was later imitated by other colleges of education.

Counts stated in a letter to Dean Russell that education rested on two foundations: psychology and social science. By focusing attention on the learning process, educational psychologists contributed to educational research and practice. However, Counts cautioned that society also had a learning process which could not be ignored by the school. He stated, American schools were often ineffective because they recognized only the laws of individual learning and disregarded the laws governing social change. An institution devoted to education could not neglect the study of forces and factors contributory to change in the social structure.[16]

In a proposal to Dean Russell, Counts urged establishment at Teachers College of an Institute of the Historical and Cultural Foundations of Education. Such an institute, formed from the regular staff members of the College, might aid in clarifying the educational ideas, policies, and practices. It would examine, reconsider, and restate the cultural and moral

values which formed the basis of social life, international relations, and education as a function of American democracy. To
understand the contemporary social order, Counts found the
reconstruction of the events of the last two and one-half centuries necessary. He advocated structuring this profound inquiry on a comprehensive and coordinated study of the historical and cultural foundations of American education. Such
inquiry would reveal the social tasks and obligations of the
schools and the spiritual and cultural resources of the American people. It would further facilitate the rational direction of
organized education during a critical period.[17]

The Institute of Historical and Cultural Foundations which
Counts proposed would compile a comprehensive bibliography
of primary sources, original studies, and basic contributions in
the fields of American cultural history and social thought, with
reference to education. It would assist in the preparation of
annals of American education, in connection with annals of
American law, government, economics, art, sciences, letters,
and religious movements. The institute would publish inacces-
sible classic works, documents, essays, and state papers relevant
to research projects and general educational research. Future
teachers were to use these materials and gain broadened knowledge of the foundations of their profession. Counts stated that
the work of the institute would not duplicate existing researches in law, economics, government, and history but would
rather consider the relation of education to such studies.[18]

Although the official history of Teachers College does not
mention an Institute of Historical and Cultural Foundations,
these areas were emphasized, and by 1938 a Department of
Social and Philosophical Foundations of Education was inaugurated as Division I of the Foundations of Education.[19]

The point to be made, however, is that Counts aided the program of broadening teacher education to include the historical and cultural foundations.

In 1931, President Butler appointed a Committee on the Relations of the University to Social Change composed of Professors Wesley C. Mitchell, Robert M. MacIver, William C. Bagley, Howard McBain, and Dean Russell. This group planned a series of studies and engaged Edmund Brunner and Florian Znaniecki as chief researchers. Although Counts was busily engaged as research director of the Commission on the Social Studies in the Schools of the American Historical Association at the time, he cooperated with this committee.[20] In January of 1931, Counts suggested the organization of an Institute of Social Research at Teachers College in a letter to Dean Russell. This proposal grew out of Counts's Inglis lecture on industrialism and secondary education, 1929. Although such an institute was not formally organized, President Butler's committee sponsored lectures and published researches on social change. Some references to Counts's letter to Russell and to his "Some Thoughts on the Organization of an Institute of Social Research at Teachers College" further illustrate Counts's efforts to broaden the program of teacher education.

Counts's proposal recommended the appointment of an advisory council of twelve men selected from Teachers College, Columbia University, and New York City. This council included Professor MacIver of the Sociology Department, Tugwell of Economics, and Llewellyn of the Law School. It also included representatives of labor and industry.[21] The institute was to be organized along the recognized subject area divisions. The staff included an economist, political scientist, lawyer, sociologist, geographer, anthropologist, social psychologist, psychiatrist, and representatives from other branches of science and thought. Each worker was expected to aid in defining and solving educational problems.[22]

Counts found educational theory enriched by fresh viewpoints which came to education by persons trained in other disciplines. He said that in the early stages of any science, large contributions were made by persons trained in several fields. He cited the example of J. Crosby Chapman, a physicist who had coauthored *The Principles of Education* with Counts. Counts added, if original and brilliant minds trained in other fields of thought could be added to the Columbia staff the outcome would be satisfactory.[23]

Counts suggested that Edmund Brunner study rural life problems.[24] He believed that education could contribute to the direction of social change in areas profoundly affected by agricultural innovation. Nowhere had an adequate educational theory been devised for the technologically transformed rural community and farming population.[25] Agricultural education in modern society was a significant educational problem.

Counts urged the political scientist to focus his research on the problems of educational control which constituted one of the most perplexing and crucial problems faced by modern education. If the school was to become a creative force, then it had to be protected from superficial and temporary demands. At the same time, it had to become more sensitive to fundamental and persistent social trends. Counts concluded that a political scientist could cast considerable light on the vital question of educational control.[26]

Since the anthropologist would exercise a broad research function, Counts found it somewhat more difficult to illustrate his area of particular investigation. The presence of an anthropologist as a member of the institute was indispensable since the study of comparative cultures was extremely illuminating in research dealing with the social function of education. Counts suggested that the anthropologist focus his research less on the existing educational forms found in different societies and more on the underlying functions performed and ideas represented.[27]

Counts also recommended the appraisal of nonscholastic educational agencies. He repeatedly warned that too many educators regarded the school as the sole and most powerful educative agency. However, other institutions such as the motion picture and radio possessed great educational potentialities which remained largely unfulfilled. He also raised the question whether the misuse of the motion picture and radio was not really an educational liability rather than an asset. Other institutions such as the family, church, and press were to be scrutinized. This inquiry would not only aid in the reconstruction of the nonscholastic agencies, but also serve to clarify the responsibility and program of the school. He concluded, the inadequacy of contemporary educational theory derived from the tendency to confine itself solely to the school.[28] Art and aesthetics also needed exploration and reorientation. Counts found the program of art too much absorbed in the individual and failing to relate to society and social affairs. He found art too little concerned with the possibilities of creating a beautiful world—beautiful factories, countrysides, and cities.[29]

In summary, Counts's proposals during the 1930s emphasized the social foundations of education—historical, sociological, political, and economic. Social research conducted by competent scholars would provide materials for the expansion of education in a socially oriented direction. With this factual and theoretical basis, teacher education might be culturally enriched and broadened.

A Proposed School of Education

The preceding discussion of Counts's emphasis on the cultural foundations of education indicated his stress on clarifying the relations between school and society. His projected definition of the school of education further completed his vision of an enlarged program of teacher preparation. For Counts, a genuine teachers college was a center of liberal culture and also instrumental in the refinement and elevation of American life.

To transform teachers colleges into institutions of liberal culture, Counts proposed a comprehensive program embracing all educational areas. Such an institution should train workers, study methods and processes, and contribute to developing programs and philosophies for all major educational agencies. He proposed a ten-fold pattern of organization which he deliniated into the college of teachers, the college of parenthood, the college of religious education, the college of journalism, the college of library service, the college of dramatics, the college of exhibits and excursions, the college of recreation, the college of adult education, and the institute of research and synthesis.

The major professional function of the college of teachers was preparing teachers and administrators for all grades and types of schools, especially public elementary and secondary schools. It also conducted practical research and experimentation to improve methods, programs, and policies.[30] Counts, at the time of the writing of this proposal in 1929, did not attack methodology as he did in the later works.

Counts stated that the college of parenthood was the most fundamental department of the school of education. This college prepared specialists in domestic relations and child nurture through systematic instruction embracing pertinent contributions of biology, psychology, psychiatry, sociology, education, and medicine. Courses were to be designed to meet the particular needs of parents.[31]

Despite decline in position and authority, Counts found the church a major educational institution. Since modern churches especially emphasized their educational functions, he recommended that the proposed college of religious education minimize dogma and emphasize sciences which solved religious problems and facilitated satisfactory adjustment to social problems. The function of the college of religious education was preparation of specialists in religious education who had critically studied the church as an educational agency.[32]

Counts also devoted attention to the operations of propaganda in mass society. Because of the important relationship between propaganda and informed political action, he had proposed an institute of propaganda analysis in *The Prospects of American Democracy*. He stated that a comprehensive school of education could not ignore the powerful educational potentiality of the press. Counts recognized a college of journalism as coordinate with the other great educational institutions. The college of journalism had a dual function: preparation of journalistic specialists and investigation of the methods, policies, and philosophy of the press.[33]

With the development of population centers, abolition of illiteracy, and rise of complex dynamic civilization, the library ranked with the press as an educational agency of prime importance. In calling for the rejection of the old tradition which made it a mere repository of books, Counts found the educational possibilities of adjusting the circulation of books to diverse individual and social needs scarcely comprehended. He stated that the development of a broad philosophy was needed to stimulate creative endeavor in librarianship on a practical level. Thus, the proposed school of education contained a college which specialized in the training of librarians and the investigation of the entire field of service represented by the library.[34]

Counts asserted that the phenomenal growth of motion pictures as a field of American entertainment made the theater a major education institution. Although retaining freedom of self-expression, the strictly educational function of drama was not to be ignored. A proper balance might be maintained, he advised, by including a college of dramatics in the education school. To him, the establishment of a college of dramatics facilitated appraisal of the theater from the view of the general welfare which provided the only kind of censorship tolerable in an intelligent and progressive society.[35]

In modern society, museums, art galleries, and exhibits increased; Counts found their educational resources only dimly realized. He believed a college of exhibits and excursions would link these various exhibits to schools, libraries, and other institutions. This required professionally trained staffs of instructors to supervise the educational activities of galleries, museums, public enterprises, and selected industrial establishments. Although modern industrial society also reduced labor expenditure, Counts believed that it increased the monotony of work and tension of life. The urban population concentration urgently necessitated the study of needed recreational facilities, playgrounds, parks, community social centers, clubs, societies, and organizations. Since these agencies performed important educational as well as recreational functions, the natural place for recreational training was in a college of recreation in a school of education.[36]

Counts also attributed the increased attention to adult education to industrial society. College extensions, correspondence courses, evening schools, lecture bureaus, musical programs, and other adult education agencies experienced rapid growth. He stated that discovery of methods and programs suited to the psychology and life conditions of the adult population was a major research problem of the college of adult education. "The development of interest in the extension of educational opportunities beyond the period of schooling and the evolution of the theory that education should be one of the chief concerns of life at all ages are the natural produce of a dynamic civilization." [37]

These nine proposed colleges of the school of education were to be coordinated by an Institute of Research and Synthesis organized in two departments: educational science and educational philosophy. While educational science prosecuted and coordinated research, educational philosophy was to develop a comprehensive theory of education in harmony with American traditions and institutions. Both of these departments would closely coordinate the activities of the institute and the other nine colleges comprising the school of education. [38]

Although this proposal for broadening the role of the school of education was made in 1929 before Counts's detailed criticism of the social function of education, it indicated a concern for integrating the school's work with that of other educative institutions. Counts had always condemned those educators who attached exaggerated importance to the school as the sole educative institution of society. He also criticized the isolation of the school from other social institutions. His proposal for a broadened educational institution in 1929 stressed these aspects rather than the promotion of a reconstructive social philosophy as did his later works. Counts's program would most likely have led to rivalry with existing schools of journalism and library science. Although he stated that the proposed departments would confine their energies to educational aspects, undoubtedly rivalry and duplication would have resulted. A more integrated means of focusing attention on the educational implications of these disciplines might have been to impress existing colleges or departments with the educational significance of their subject fields. Courses and individuals expert in education might have been added and a greater degree of coordination attained within the existing institutions.

Counts's major emphasis was developing an interdisciplinary approach to educational problems. Both his emphasis on the educational foundations and the broadened program of the teacher training institution reflected this interdisciplinary method which drew materials relevant to education from a number of disciplines. He suggested that scholars in fields other than education be called upon for consultation and advice. His own approach to social and educational analysis used sociological, psychological, historical, philosophical, and other findings relevant to education.

Responsibilities of the Teacher

After urging the broadening of the teacher education program, Counts discussed the role of the teacher in American society. Although the teacher was to be a master of his specialty, he should also be cognizant of the larger ends to which his specialty was directed. Counts urged teachers to participate in community life, identify with democracy, and cherish humanity. As an active member of his profession, the teacher was to devote time and energy to the advancing of public education.

This socially oriented teacher was to be produced by placing emphasis on the social, cultural, and philosophical foundations of education.[39]

In *Dare the School Build a New Social Order?*, Counts urged teachers to deliberately seek and use power in the interests of the popular masses. Representing the common and abiding interests of the people, teachers were under social obligation to protect and advance these popular aspirations.[40] A society needing leadership might accept guidance by teachers who were scientists and scholars at all levels. Through powerful organizations, teachers could influence public sentiments and seek to direct educational policies.[41] To the extent that they fashioned the curriculum and procedures of the school, teachers could influence social attitudes, ideals, and behavior.

To gain some degree of power, Counts called upon teachers to do four things: one, develop a social orientation to education; two, combat the tendency to aristocracy; three, ally themselves with the masses; and four, organize a comprehensive professional organization. Counts had always stressed the cultural and social implications of education in American civilization. Teachers, he said, needed to understand fully American civilization's historical and world setting. This required sensitivity to the moral implications of the teacher's social role. Counts called upon teachers to narrow the gap between school and society: "Education as a force for social reconstruction must march hand in hand with the living and creative forces of the social order." [42]

Counts's social interpretation of contemporary American society revealed his fears of the growth of the economic aristocracy. Teachers, he cautioned, must be ever alert to detect and oppose minority attempts to dictate school policy. When reactionary forces controlled the school, the school served the dominant classes and prolonged social conflict. Urging teachers to resist all pressure groups, he stated that teachers must insist that the educational program be conceived and administered in terms of the general welfare and not in the interests of the concentrated power of an economic elite of wealth and privilege.[43]

The Committee of the Progressive Education Association on Social and Economic Problems agreed with Counts and stated:

> If the teachers are to play a positive and creative role in building a better social order, indeed, if they are not to march in the ranks of economic, political, and cultural reaction, they will have to emancipate themselves completely from the domination of the business interests of the nation, cease cultivating the manners and associations of bankers and promotion agents, repudiate utterly the ideal of material success as the goal of education, abandon the smug middle-class tradition on which they have been nourished in the past, acquire a realistic understanding of the forces that actually rule the world, and formulate a fundamental program of thought and action that will deal honestly and intelligently with the problems of industrial civilization.[44]

In *Social Frontier,* Counts urged teachers to support the conception of social welfare which served the many rather than the few. He called upon them to substitute human rights for property rights, democratic collectivism for an oligarchic economic individualism, and social planning for anarchy and chaos. Further, teachers were to develop in the population values, attitudes, ideals, and loyalties consistent with the emergent life pattern.[45] *A Call to the Teachers of the Nation* stated that teachers' loyalties should go to the great body of the laboring population—to farmers and industrial workers.[46]

Counts urged teachers to form a comprehensive professional organization. To participate in building a new social order, teachers needed effective organization. Counts cautioned that the desired organizational goal would not be reached until the entire membership of the profession was united into a single great body fully equipped to fight the battles of teachers and to represent education in community, state, and nation. The process of organization involved the mastering of the arts of publicity, massing of financial resources, ability to deal with government and private interests, and establishing of procedures for cases involving freedom and tenure.[47]

Counts apparently advocated organization of teachers into an organizational pattern corresponding to that of the great labor unions. He was especially active in the American Federation of Teachers and served as its president from 1939 until 1942. In accepting this office, he outlined an eight-point program for the federation which might serve as an illustration of the kind of organization which he favored: one, cultivation of the spirit of independence, critical judgment, and leadership; two, open membership to all teachers; three, analysis and evaluation of all political programs but commitment to the federation rather than to political parties; four, removal of all racial, religious, political, or other such discrimination and an emphasis on tenure based on merit; five, mobilization of funds to defend teachers unjustly dismissed or deprived of rights; six, expansion of the services of the national organization; seven, integration in the *American Teacher,* the journal of the federation, of the practical and theoretical interests of teachers; and eight, active cultivation of friendship between the American Federation of Teachers and the American Federation of Labor.[48]

Summation

In summary, it can be stated that Counts urged a broadened program of teacher education which emphasized the cultural foundations and related the school to the other social institutions. He also urged a comprehensive organization of teachers and the seeking of power by this organization on behalf of democratic collectivism. Of these two suggestions, the first was eventually accepted by American education and the patterns of teacher education were broadened and enriched. The second suggestion of organizational methods is still much debated in educational circles. Although some advocate teacher organization along the lines of the major labor unions, still others such as the National Education Association urge teacher organization along broader professional lines.

Counts also believed that teachers were capable of exercising power in the advance of social reconstruction. Some, like Agnes de Lima, argued that the teachers were unlikely to advance social change since they had as a class been trained to social docility and economically protected by life tenure of office.[49] If economics were as significant as suggested by Counts in his earlier analysis, it seemed unlikely that the teachers could escape their middle class bias and join with the lower economic classes to further democratic collectivism.

1. George S. Counts, *The Social Foundations of Education* (New York: Charles Scribner's Sons, 1934), p. 273.

2. Counts, "What Is a School of Education?", *Teachers College Record,* 30 (1929), 648.

3. Counts, *Social Foundations,* p. 275.

4. Ibid., p. 276.

5. Ibid., p. 277.

6. Ibid., p. 276.

7. Ibid., pp. 557–58.

8. George S. Counts, "Proposed Study of Education and Culture in an American Industrial Community," in the private library of George S. Counts, Carbondale, Illinois, p. 10.

9. Counts, *Social Foundations,* pp. 4–5.

10. Ibid., p. 5.

11. Counts, "Secondary Education and the Social Problem," *School Executives Magazine,* 51 (1932), 520.

12. Committee of the Progressive Education Association on Social and Economic Problems, *A Call to the Teachers of the Nation* (New York: John Day Co., 1932), p. 25.

13. Lawrence A. Cremin, David A. Shannon, and Mary E. Townsend, *A History of Teachers College, Columbia University* (New York: Columbia University Press, 1954), p. 144.

14. Ibid., p. 146.

15. Ibid., p. 145.

16. George S. Counts to Dean William F. Russell, January 19, 1931, in the private library of George S. Counts, Carbondale, Illinois, p. 4.

17. George S. Counts, "A Proposal for Historical and Cultural Foundations at Columbia," in the private library of George S. Counts, pp. 5–6.

18. Ibid., pp. 7–8.

19. Cremin et al., *History of Teachers College,* p. 158.

20. Ibid., p. 144.

21. George S. Counts, "Tentative Plan for the Organization of an Institute of Social Research at Teachers College," in the private library of George S. Counts, Carbondale, Illinois, p. 2. (Counts stated that this proposal was written in the early 1930s when he referred to it in the letter of January 19, 1931, to Dean Russell.)

22. George S. Counts, "Some Thoughts on the Organization of an Institute of Social Research at Teachers College," in the private library of George S. Counts, Carbondale, Illinois, p. 10.

23. Letter to Dean Russell, p. 1.

24. Ibid., p. 3.

25. Ibid.

26. Ibid.

27. Ibid.

28. Ibid., p. 4.

29. Ibid.

30. Counts, "What Is a School of Education?", p. 649.

31. Ibid., p. 650.

32. Ibid.

33. Ibid., p. 651.

34. Ibid.

35. Ibid., p. 652.

36. Ibid., pp. 652–53.

37. Ibid., p. 653.

38. Ibid., p. 654.

39. Counts, *The Prospects of American Democracy* (New York: John Day Co., 1938), p. 346.

40. Counts, *Dare the School Build a New Social Order?* (New York: John Day Co., 1932), p. 29.

41. Ibid., p. 28.

42. Ibid., pp. 30–31.

43. Counts, *Prospects,* p. 310.

44. *Call to the Teachers,* p. 20.

45. "The Position of the *Social Frontier,*" *Social Frontier,* 1 (1935), 31.

46. *Call to the Teachers,* pp. 19–20.

47. Counts, *Prospects,* p. 312.

48. Counts, "Rally Around the AFT Program," *American Teacher,* 24 (1939), 2.

49. Agnes A. de Lima, "Education—For What?", *New Republic,* 71 (1932), 317.

VIII. Proposed Educational Program

Counts's social analysis during the 1930s suggested the outline of a program of political action to curb the growth of economic aristocracy and restore the equalitarian economic and social bases of the American life. After analyzing the American educational system, he suggested an educational program to promote a collective democracy that contained five major emphases: one, a program of education based upon the cultural heritage; two, a reconstruction of the heritage in terms of emergent democratic collectivism; three, deliberate imposition of democratic collectivism in the schools; four, a curriculum design emphasizing social knowledge; and five, a broadened and enriched program of teacher education and organization. These five major emphases contained the heart of Counts's educational proposals during the 1930s. Each of these has been examined in some detail in the earlier discussion. It is proposed to conclude this section of the paper concerning Counts's educational theory with a brief examination of the content of the social knowledge and a discussion of the value criteria associated with democratic collectivism.

Popular Education and the Twelve-Year Common School

Counts believed a program of popular education was essential to preserve free institutions and democratic processes. A common, popular education diminished the possibilities of a cultural separation between the masses and the leaders. Further, the twelve-year common school had advanced popular education by obliterating traditional distinctions between elementary and secondary education and establishing a unified educational program. Counts urged that popular education provide foundational training in social attitudes, dispositions, and powers designed to advance emergent collectivism.[1]

Public education should promote the common good rather than further egoistic and selfish impulses to individual aggrandizement. The common school was not designed to raise selected individuals out of their class to positions of exploitation. Rather, Counts found the twelve-year common school to be a powerful democratic instrument which was motivated by devotion to the common good.

Counts presented a program which emphasized eight major areas of social knowledge. To preserve and develop democratic values, knowledge had to be selected and organized according to the criteria of democratic collectivism. Although serving a definite purpose, this knowledge was to be subjected to the most critical scholarship. Counts listed the major areas of social knowledge to be presented by popular education: nature and history of man; history of American democracy; rise of industrial society; contemporary American social structure; social ideas, philosophies, and programs; agencies and methods of propaganda; and purposes and potentialities of American democracy. To elaborate the general content of this socially oriented program, discussion of each of these areas of social knowledge follows.

First, Counts stated that the school was to provide a broad account of the nature and history of man. Combining anthropology, sociology, history, economics, and political science, this account included discussion of man's special traits and powers, struggle with physical environment, migrations, and differentiation into races and peoples. It devoted attention to the history of invention, discovery, advances in hunting, agriculture, and industry, and founding of social and political institutions. This account was to conclude with a study of the world distribution of natural resources and populations, patterns of cultural diversity, national boundaries, and relations of people. The aim of this appraisal was the gaining of experience, the evaluation of the heritage, and the viewing of contemporary problems in rational perspective.[2]

Second, Counts urged presentation of the history of American democracy, tracing its origins back through the centuries of Western history. It should be viewed and studied in its various economic, social, cultural, and political aspects. As suggested in the previous discussion of this area in the chapter on the curriculum, Counts's proposal for the study of American democracy resembled his own analysis of the American cultural heritage. The equalitarian origins of American democracy were to be emphasized; the tradition of economic individualism was to be treated as an archaic residue destined for erosion by the forces of industrialization.

Third, the school was to trace the origins of industrial society from the beginning of the industrial revolution to the present. As Counts had stressed industrial civilization in his frame of reference for social analysis, so did he emphasize it in his educational program. This emphasis, which illustrated the cultural and social aspects of industrialism, was intended to inspire a respect for work and to acquaint the young with the myriad vocational possibilities found in an industrial society.

Fourth, Counts urged that the school provide a clear and bold analysis of the contemporary American social structure. The major aim was the revelation of emergent class and political patterns. Information on wealth and income, relations of economic groups to tools of production, sentiments, loyalties, and traditions, and extent of fundamental community among various groups were to be studied. Students were to investigate the position of the dominant economic class, government, press, radio, motion picture, school, and church. Specifically revealing his economic predilections, Counts urged the study of economic man, the natural economic order, the profit motive, market and price system, free enterprise, laissez-faire, and inheritance.[3] This proposed study of American society was a largely economic analysis and reflected his predilection to economic conditioning during the 1930s.

Fifth, Counts stated that the school should encourage students to analyze crucial contradictions, conflicts, and maladjustments in contemporary society. He listed some of these contradictions as between historic capitalistic individualism and the close integration of industrial economy; between private enterprise and the social operations of production; between planlessness, irrationality, and uncertainty and the planfulness, rationality, and precision of technology; between inherited conceptions of natural economic laws and the necessity of social control; between democracy and economic aristocracy; and finally between nationalism and the trend toward world inte-

gration.[4] From these contradictions and conflicts arose the maladjustments which threatened to throw mankind backward
into chronic depression or conflict. If American democracy was
to survive, Counts stated that action was necessary to resolve
these contradictions and conflicts.[5] His suggested area of the
contradictions and maladjustments prevalent in contemporary
American society revealed somewhat more clearly the nature
of his proposed imposition. These conflicts were to be examined on the basis of their agreement or contradiction with the
collectivistic interpretation of American history. This study
was to define clearly for the younger generation the conflict
in American society between two divergent concepts of the
heritage.

Sixth, Counts recommended that the school critically expose students to various social ideas, philosophies, and programs competing for mastery in the world. Although no effort
should be made to enforce narrow indoctrination, this examination was to have a definite orientation. Every system was to
be evaluated in terms of democratic and industrial potentialities. Although some of these systems might make useful contributions, the American civilization was conditioned by the
peculiar history, circumstances, loyalties, and opportunities of
the American people.[6] Thus, the student was not left to examine these diverse social theories without a means of comparison as a guide. Democratic collectivism once again provided the yardstick with which to approach this examination.

Seventh, the program of popular education was to thoroughly acquaint the rising generation with the actual theories
and methods of propaganda. In his program of political action,
Counts discussed the great potentialities of the mass media as
a formative influence. He cautioned against the domination
by the economic aristocracy over the tools of propaganda. Both

The Prospects of American Democracy (1938) and *The Schools Can Teach Democracy* (1939) urged an understanding of the mass media. At this time, Nazi Germany made great use of propaganda to influence its people to accept dictatorship. Counts also had witnessed the Soviet use of propaganda to mold opinion on behalf of the regime. He stated that the successful employment of the democratic processes depended upon making the ordinary citizen conscious and critical of propaganda. Unless the public became sophisticated in dealing with the mass media, public opinion, the foundation of political democracy, would be corrupted and the superstructure of free institutions jeopardized. Since the citizen was to analyze the motives and purposes of the propagandist, the school should systematically and comprehensively equip the rising generation to use the scientific method in facing social problems and in interpreting the pronouncements of the mass media. The role of propaganda was to be included in the historical account with reference to critical periods in the American past and to the practices of current dictatorships. The student was to be aware of the use of symbols, manipulation of loyalties, appeals to prejudice, and the suppression and distortion of facts.[7]

Eight, the school was to develop a challenging conception of the purposes and potentialities of democracy in the United States and in the world.[8] This embodied a faith in the democratic processes, a vision of the good society, a sense of social responsibility, and an orientation to democratic collectivism. Since all of Counts's efforts were directed to this end, little elaboration of this point is needed.

Thus, Counts's program of popular education rested primarily in the areas of history and the social sciences. He did not suggest adding specific courses to the curriculum but rather recommended an outline of the topics which were to become part of the program of popular education. Where possible, these areas were to be incorporated within the existing curricular design. The general orientation and approach to the educational program was the most significant aspect. In the chapter on the curriculum, the specific method of presentation was indicated. Students were to move from the near to the remote, from the present to the past along the general patterns suggested by Dewey's second level of curriculum.

Although Counts stressed the social orientation of subject matter, this did not constitute the sole educational program. The mathematical, scientific, artistic, and linguistic areas were also a part of the educational program. Counts suggested a program of popular education which served as a general education for all the people to build a common core of knowledge and values essential to the emergent age of democratic collectivism. Thus far, in the program of education, the content areas of the program have been discussed. Along with these bodies of facts and data, Counts also advocated a specific kind of value orientation which was equally important in bringing about the common core of shared belief suggested by the program of popular education.

Popular Education and Democratic Values

Throughout his works, Counts indicated the kind of value preference which he regarded as essential for the coming age of democratic collectivism. He rejected those values associated with the old order of economic individualism. In contrast, he emphasized cooperation, coordination, devotion to the common good, and democracy. The order of values suggested by

Counts fell into four major orders: one, the equalitarian; two, the critically democratic; three, collectivistic; and, four, individualistic.

First of all, Counts's educational program stressed equalitarian values. Returning to his analysis of the American cultural heritage, Counts had emphasized the agrarian-frontier spirit of equality. Political democracy rested, said Counts, on a society of equal men. He felt American democracy especially threatened by the rise of an economic aristocracy which bred the spirit of inequality. For Counts, the educational program was to rear the young in the spirit and program of equality. The American cultural heritage was to be examined in the schools to allow students to find and trace the roots of equality in the American experience. The recognition of the supreme worth of the individual led inevitably to the principle of equality among the members of society. With each individual regarded as uniquely precious, there could be no moral support for the existence of privileged orders.

The school was to develop in the individual a profound allegiance to the principles of human equality, brotherhood, dignity, and worth. No individual was to be permitted to discriminate or to be discriminated against because of race, family, nationality, politics, or religion. The ideals of free society were to be brought to the student's level of consciousness.[9] In *Education and American Civilization* (1952) Counts urged that particular attention should be paid to children from economically and culturally deprived groups; children from all occupational, cultural, religious, and racial groups were to be brought together in the common school.[10]

In urging equalitarianism, Counts never recommended an equal level of mediocrity. Differences were to be valued and encouraged in an attitude of mutual respect. The school, while adhering to the conception of equality, was to impress upon the rising generation the imperative necessity of recognizing and placing in positions of trust and responsibility persons of talent, virtue, and training.[11] In understanding the principle of equality, Counts warned that utopianism was to be avoided. Rather, each, within the limits of his powers, was entitled to the same rights, liberties, and opportunities, and was subject to the same duties and responsibilities.[12] Counts was really urging devotion to the principle of equality of opportunity.

Second, Counts associated the democratic processes with the development of the experimental temper of critical mindedness. He believed that the genuinely critical mind was one of the most important resources of free society. Such a mind was to be highly disciplined and armed with knowledge and understanding. The use of the democratic processes depended on the development of the intellectual virtues of accuracy, precision, truthfulness, open-mindedness, and absolute integrity.[13]

The school was to arouse deep loyalties to the process of free discussion, criticism, and group decision which were the life blood of the democratic method. A mistrust of authoritarianism was to be cultivated and decisions were to be based on rational foundations. Counts warned against the abuse of the process of discussion and criticism which undermined confidence in the democratic process. Delaying tactics, refusal to abide by majority will, and conspiracy threatened the moral foundations of popular government. Therefore, all criticism must be informed and honest. The school, Counts added, was to inculcate a healthy skepticism toward all final and complete solutions to social problems and cultivate a healthy regard for the scientific method in the area of social problems.[14]

Counts recommended that the scientific method be used to approach the historical, sociological, and economic materials included in the program of popular education. In advocating the use of the scientific method in social analysis, he cautioned against complete detachment and urged that the hypotheses be genuinely tested. He stated that in abstract theory, experimentalism took on the guise of complete reasonableness and provoked a sympathetic response in the mind of every thoughtful man. However, he asked:

> Who could take exception to the doctrine that in social relations, as in the sphere of natural phenomena, conclusions should be tentatively held and the intellect should never be closed to new revelations from experience?

> The difficulty arises out of the fact that new revelations are created as often as discovered and the further fact that in social experimentation the materials of the experiment must at the same time give it direction.[15]

Therefore, Counts recommended materials of instruction that contributed to the directions of experiment along the general framework of democratic collectivism. Although his critics challenged that this imposition violated the experimentalist criteria of open-endedness, Counts argued that a frame of reference was necessary to guide youth into the area of social experimentation for the emergent age.

Third, Counts recommended the cultivation of those values which contributed to the building of a cooperative morality. In developing his educational theory, he stressed the importance of group life. For him, society implied group life, and group life implied cooperation and mutual aid. As the processes of technology and industrialization transformed American life, a new morality had to be developed which showed greater concern for and devotion to the general welfare. In his analysis of traditional education, Counts found that the motive of individual success backed by material rewards was often the driving force in the education of the young. This individualistic emphasis reflected the outmoded legacy of economic individualism which defined liberty as the right of the individual to concentrate all efforts on personal aggrandizement. Counts warned that if the various groups which existed in the pluralistic American society lacked a common conception of the general welfare, separate and conflicting moralities would develop.[16]

In his proposed popular program of education, Counts urged that the young become familiar with the rise of industrial civilization and the emergent collectivistic age. He also found it necessary to go beyond mere comprehension to the development of habits and dispositions. The young were to be exposed to cooperative undertakings, organizational work, and social planning. In the formation of cooperative values, a sense of loyalty to the total community was to be cultivated instead of narrow interests. The educational program was to be permeated with concern for the general welfare.[17] Counts stressed the crucial role of education in building a new morality. Unless habits, attitudes, ideas, and dispositions of the people were altered, the new social order would never appear.[18]

Despite Counts's emphasis on collectivistic values, he continued to stress the dignity of each individual as a uniquely different personality. Educational opportunity was an individual right which could not be denied in a truly democratic society. In *Education and American Civilization* (1952) he stated that the huge establishments of industry and government, the vast population concentrations, and the mass organizations of economics and politics so characteristic of the industrial age often overwhelmed individuals with a sense of insignificance and helplessness. This tendency to mass organization invited the political, intellectual, and personal disfranchisement of the common people and the usurping of power by some dictator or oligarchy. In the modern era, the deliberate cultivation of individual excellence was a crucial and urgent responsibility of democratic education.[19]

At first glance, there may seem to be a contradiction between Counts's advocacy of both collectivistic and individualistic values. Counts, himself, recognized no conflict between the two. Rather, he structured what might be thought of as two planes of values. One of these areas of value centered in the material realm, especially in the economic area. He conceived of an intimate relation between economic condition and equality of opportunity. Unless a society was willing to share its material wealth and resources among all of its citizens to the degree that equality of opportunity became a reality, then certain individuals, lacking the necessary material supports, would be denied the opportunity to develop in the individual realm of values. In other words, a new morality had to be achieved relative to the area of quantitative material supports which would free men of the fears and pressures of survival. During the depression era, in particular, many theorists focused their pleas on an argument to increase the quantitative area of democracy, the greater sharing of the material supports of life.

Counts believed that a more comprehensive sharing of the quantitative or material supports of life, especially in the economic area, would free men to attain greater expression in the more individualistic areas of art, literature, and science. He did not believe that equality in the quantitative area would necessarily constrict the opportunities for growth and achievement in the spiritual, nonmaterial, or qualitative area. Further, he held that the very nature of democracy demanded a recognition of the uniqueness of the individual human personality, itself a form of individualism. Unfortunately, the two areas of quantitative and qualitative values were often blurred by the existent set of values based on economic individualism. Critics of social and economic individualism necessarily meant the restriction of individualism in the other areas of life. Counts disagreed with these critics. He believed that only social and economic planning could free man from economic fear, privation, and inequality of opportunity. Once a quantitative sharing or a greater measure of equality was achieved and extended to the area of educational opportunity, then man could grow in the areas of art, literature, science, and philosophy. Greater areas of individualism in the qualitative realm could be achieved.

To further explore this seeming contradiction between collectivistic and individualistic values, it is necessary to return to Counts's emphasis on the cultural or group heritage. For him, the individual achieved freedom as he acquired the group values through associative life. Cultural tools and skills, symbolic and linguistic, were derived from group experience. As man contributed to group welfare, he achieved further growth and greater freedom. Counts rejected any notion that man achieved freedom only as he was separated from group life. Rather, the full measure of individual maturity was achieved as the individual assumed all the responsibilities of adult life—economic, familial, civic, and religious.[20]

Counts believed that the United States possessed the quantitative raw materials, natural and economic resources, to produce a rich and varied civilization in the qualitative area, the nonmaterial realm of human life. Only as American society recognized and accepted the responsibility to share this quantitative area fully among all men could individual men realize themselves fully in the qualitative area. Counts believed this responsibility could be achieved only as individuals acted in accord with value preferences conditioned by a commitment to a pattern of collective democracy.

The development in the individual of a feeling of competence and adequacy was the primary obligation of democratic education. To Counts, the success of democracy was measured in terms of its liberation of human personality. Democratic education was to war on the conditions which blocked men from achieving full physical, intellectual and moral growth. Public education was to reject all systems of measurement, classification, or instruction that submerged the individual or placed him in a fixed quantitative relationship.[21] The school was held responsible to bring each individual to the fullest realization of his moral, intellectual, physical, and artistic potentialities.

To achieve moral maturity, each individual had to assume the role of a responsible member of society. In adjusting to the natural and social environment, man was required to bring his impulses under purposeful direction, to subordinate the smaller to the greater good, the immediate to the distant, and the individual to the social. In American society, this meant building moral commitment into youth. In a democracy, the young had to acquire democratic values through self-discipline. Each individual, under careful guidance, was to undertake those projects and assignments which eventually would lead him to learning experiences independent of the teacher. For Counts, self-direction in the light of social responsibility was the ultimate test of the education of a liberally educated and free man.[22]

As the individual experienced the mediating influence of culture, Counts stated that he developed his intellectual abilities, desire for knowledge, and power of reasoning. The fullest development of these powers was one of the supreme purposes of organized education in a democracy. Language, number, and scientific method were essential to the achievement of intellectual maturity.[23] In addition to intellectual maturity Counts found physical excellence a necessary ingredient in fulfilling man's potentiality for growth. A program of health education was needed to discover and correct remedial physical defects and to form proper habits of diet, work, play, and rest. In other words, Counts urged the development of both physical and intellectual potentialities.[24]

Finally, Counts stated that the individual achieved human stature in the fullest sense only as he developed artistic powers and aesthetic sensitivity. A complete education was to develop creative and appreciative powers both as a social resource and as an individual personal possession. In modern industrial society, with mass characteristics and tendencies toward regimentation, the emphasis on individuality assumed a special urgency.[25]

Education for a Civilization of Beauty and Grandeur

In *Education and American Civilization* (1952) Counts stated that the United States possessed the material, spiritual, intellectual, and moral resources necessary to fashion an education for a civilization of beauty and grandeur. The central purpose of economic and political institutions, he said, was to provide the material base and social conditions essential to releasing and fulfilling the creative powers of man. Technological advance created opportunities for an almost unlimited advance and refinement of American civilization. The wealth of the new society could easily be harnessed for creating genuine equality of educational opportunity for all children and even for all adults. Although industrial civilization greatly enlarged and complicated the educational task, it immeasurably increased the institutional resources through which the responsibility of rearing the young and enlightening the old could be discharged.[26] Finally, he repeated the plea which he made during the depression period of the 1930s. A great education, he said, required a great and noble purpose. It must be guided by a noble conception of life and civilization. Such a conception should embrace the best in the American heritage, confront the revolutionary forces and conditions of the contemporary world, and take into account the vast technical potentialities of the industrial age.[27]

Counts's Educational Theory Restated

In conclusion, a restatement of Counts's educational theory and program serves to illustrate his contribution to American education. Primarily, he urged that the educational program be based upon a searching analysis of civilization. He urged an educational theory which recognized the emergent reality of the age, democratic collectivism. Although traditionally American education repudiated any deliberate attempts at indoctrination, Counts advocated that the schools build a new social order along the very general contours of democratic collectivism. To accomplish this task, a deliberate program of imposition and commitment was necessary.

Counts's curriculum design was culturally and socially oriented and emphasized history and the social sciences. Current social conflicts were to be investigated. Before any action was

taken by students, the relevant conclusions of the various social disciplines were to be studied and mastered. Although he
urged the use of the experimental method of science in the
study of social knowledge, he did not encourage attempts to
subordinate recognized subject matter areas. Through the
schools, knowledge and values relative to advancing democratic
collectivism would ensue.

After examination of the American educational heritage,
Counts stated that deliberate social planning seemed highly
unlikely in the existent educational system which was decentralized and dominated by favored social groups interested in
perpetuating the status quo. Therefore, he turned to the teachers to build a new social order. Teachers needed preparation
for this task by a broadened and enriched program of teacher
education and a more militant and highly organized comprehensive professional organization.

Counts found education was always particular to a given
civilization at a certain developmental stage. According to this
view of cultural relativism, his educational program during
the 1930s was relevant to a society plagued by social problems,
economic depression, and mass unemployment. Lack of faith
both in the political and economic systems prevailed. Counts
formulated an educational philosophy and program which was
conditioned by the depression-ridden climate of opinion.

Counts's educational theory and program as formulated in
the 1930s attempted to analyze social conflicts rather than to
immediately cure them. Perhaps, he felt analysis might lead
to eventual cure. His program, rich in social and historical materials, would have produced individuals skilled in social analysis and with a keen understanding of their society. If this proposed educational program had been fulfilled in its entirety, it
may have even produced confirmed democratic collectivists.

However, Counts's program of education was not carried out on any great scale through organized public support. In fact, by the time that he had definitely formulated an educational program in response to the depression, the winds of change were beginning to sweep away the emphasis on economics and problems of unemployment. When he published *The Prospects of American Democracy* (1938) and *The Schools Can Teach Democracy* (1939), attention was already being focused on the international situation and the possibility of another world war. Since education reflected a particular civilization at a definite time in history, Counts, as educator, too, shifted his attention to the international scene and was recognized as an authority on Soviet education.

The works of Counts and other like-minded scholars emphasized the social aspects of education. Counts was only one of many who advocated the increased role of the social studies, however. Undoubtedly, the work of persons such as Harold Rugg also influenced the increased attention to social problems. Counts played a considerable role in broadening the patterns of teacher education to include a more direct focus on the cultural and social foundations of education. But here too, he was joined by men of similar mode such as William H. Kilpatrick, John L. Childs, and Boyd H. Bode.

In almost all educational histories and in many intellectual histories, Counts is mentioned. He was, it seems, a spokesman for an age and a climate of opinion. He spoke the words that many wanted to say but could not find. His colorful, and sometimes evangelistic language pleaded the causes and voiced the demands of the long neglected American teacher. However, Counts had still a greater lasting achievement than that of spokesman.

Counts popularized a mode of analysis upon which to base

educational philosophy and program, the civilizational approach to education. In its mechanics, the theorist must use an interdisciplinary methodology to analyze the civilization and to locate the emergent tendencies of the age in light of the contemporary realities. Rooted in the particular culture, the emergent tendencies are reconstructed in terms of the cultural heritage in order to fashion a social and hence educational philosophy and program. This civilizational philosophy of education can never be fixed, nor become static, since civilization is always changing and variable. Although this investigation was rooted in the language and history of the 1930s, certain elements in Counts's theory can be applied to contemporary society. The democratic heritage and technological civilization are still major cornerstones of educational and social programs. Counts's call in the 1930s inspired many educators and scholars to examine the cultural context of education and to suggest educational means to be used in building a new social order.

1. George S. Counts, *The Prospects of American Democracy* (New York: John Day Co., 1938), pp. 323–24.

2. Ibid., pp. 330–31.

3. Ibid., p. 334.

4. Ibid., pp. 334–35.

5. Counts, *The Schools Can Teach Democracy* (New York: John Day Co., 1939), p. 27.

6. Ibid., p. 28.

7. Ibid., pp. 28–29.

8. Counts, *Prospects,* p. 337.

9. Counts, *Schools Can Teach Democracy,* p. 18.

10. Counts, *Education and American Civilization* (New York: Bureau of Publications, Teachers College, Columbia University, 1952), p. 340.

11. Counts, *Schools Can Teach Democracy*, p. 20.

12. Counts, *Education and American Civilization*, pp. 331–32.

13. Counts, *Education and the Foundations of Human Freedom*, (Pittsburgh: University of Pittsburgh Press, 1962), p. 83.

14. Counts, *Schools Can Teach Democracy*, pp. 19–20.

15. Counts, *The Soviet Challenge to America* (New York: John Day Co., 1931), p. 326.

16. Counts, *Education and American Civilization*, p. 381.

17. Counts, *Education and the Promise of America* (New York: Macmillan Co., 1946).

18. Counts, *Soviet Challenge*, p. 66.

19. Counts, *Education and American Civilization*, p. 313.

20. Counts, *Education and the Promise*, p. 119.

21. Counts, *The Schools Can Teach Democracy*, pp. 17–18.

22. Counts, *Education and American Civilization*, p. 325.

23. Counts, *Education and the Promise*, pp. 115–16.

24. Ibid., p. 115.

25. Ibid., pp. 118–19.

26. Counts, *Education and American Civilization*, pp. 299–300.

27. Ibid., p. 308.

IX. Counts and Marxism

In *The Transformation of the School,* Lawrence Cremin prefaced his discussion of Counts's "Dare Progressive Education Be Progressive?" with a brief critique. According to Cremin, Counts's evaluation of progressivism in American education followed two lines: one, partly Marxian; the other, partly reminiscent of the traditional progressive critique of capitalism.[1] It would seem that an analysis of the origins or well-springs of Counts's social and educational position might be developed along these two lines of thought: Marxism and progressivism. Counts's position will be examined in a Marxian context and then located within the framework of American social reformism. No attempt will be made to analyze Marxian theory but rather the emphasis will be placed on a comparison and contrast of Counts's position in relation to Marxism.

Marxism and Counts

When in the 1930s Counts proposed an educational program committed to democratic collectivism, he was accused of advocating Marxism. Harold L. Varney attacked Counts as an evil genius of *Social Frontier* group who was determined to radicalize American youth through indoctrination in the schools. Varney accused Counts of being sympathetic to communism and of using a Marxian social interpretation in his educational writing.[2] The Hearst press and some critics also alleged that Counts was plotting to transfer the Marxian revolution and the classless society to America. It has previously been stated in this paper that Counts had no sympathy for communism in either the Soviet Union or in the United States. In Chapter 3, "Educational Responses to the 1930s," it was pointed out that: one, Counts recognized Soviet planning as a challenge to the United States but never recommended emulation of Soviet communism in the United States; two, he opposed communist infiltration of the American Federation of Teachers; three, he regarded Soviet foreign policies as a menace to world peace. Therefore, this section will not deal with communism as an activist political movement but will rather concentrate on the theoretical implications of Marxism in relation to Counts's stated social and educational position.

The interpretation which follows will provide evidence that Counts regarded Marxism as simply another totalitarian philosophy which negated the democratic ethic. A consideration of specific aspects of Marxism in relation to Counts's social and educational position will further document this point. The following areas of traditional Marxism will be considered: dialectical materialism, economic determinism, the role of surplus value, class conflict, and the role of revolution.

Dialectical Materialism

Marxian dialectical materialism incorporated the Hegelian dialectic with the materialism of man's social and physical environment. For Hegel, the dialectic was accompanied by ceaseless successions of ideological conflicts. Every idea embodied a partial truth and also contained an antithesis, an opposite, or contradiction to the partial truth. From the conflict of thesis and antithesis emerged a newer conflict and tension. Utilizing the dialectical formula of thesis, antithesis, and synthesis, the process continued until comprehensive unification occurred in the Absolute Idea. Marx placed the dialectical process in the realm of the physical and material. Instead of a conflict of ideas, Marx used dialectical materialism to interpret political, social, and particularly economic history. The history of man was a struggle between conflicting economic classes. Marx believed the laws of history were contained in a single, nonrepetitive process embodied in the formula of dialectical materialism. Instead of the Hegelian Absolute, Marx postulated the classless society as the final and, hence, absolute fulfillment of the dialectical process.

Resting upon dialectical materialism, Marxian social philosophy proposed a closed or deterministic interpretation of history and social change. All human development was encased in the determined scheme of events and followed a definite pattern. Nowhere in Counts's social interpretation did the dialectical pattern emerge—not in the Hegelian sense nor in the Marxian sense. Grounded in the empiricism and experimental method of instrumentalism, Counts rejected any adherence to a completely deterministic system of thought and action. He did not attempt to formulate any universal laws of historical and social change as did Marx. Two essential patterns of thought militated against his acceptance of a universal system of historical causation: one, cultural relativism; two, emphasis on human responsibility for social action.

Counts believed that every society possessed unique and peculiar life and thought patterns. These patterns required a particular examination of the historical origins of any particular group. Although American society shared the heritage of Western civilization, it possessed its own peculiar developmental pattern which was inexplicable by any set of universal laws of social change such as those of Marxian dialectical materialism. To Counts, the forces operative in American civilization such as democracy and technology could only be explained in terms of a particular historical perspective. Since education was conditioned by a particular society at a given time and place, it, too, could be understood only in terms of a peculiar evolutionary and historical pattern.

Counts was further convinced that man was responsible for his actions, both individually and collectively. He believed that human intelligence given free rein might determine social purpose and control action to achieve the aims embodied in the purpose. One, if organized education deliberately exposed students to areas of social problems and conflict, a body of social knowledge would be acquired by the students. Two, this body of social knowledge was structured in terms of the conflict areas of contemporary society. Three, these conflicts were to be considered in the light of the reality of the heritage, democracy; and the reality of industrial civilization, technology. Four, social conflict and contradiction required resolution; hu-

man intelligence would experimentally formulate hypotheses
of action to resolve these areas of conflict. Five, appropriate action in light of the experimentally determined purposes would
be the means of man's own self-determination. Counts conceived this as an "open-ended process" whose only limits were
subject to free intelligence. Therefore, Marx's reliance on dialectical materialism and Counts's rejection of predetermined
historical laws constituted a crucial difference between the
two positions.

For Hegel, the more inclusive the Idea, the greater the unfolding of the Absolute. For Marx, the nearer the proximity
to the eventual realization of the classless society, the greater
the degree of human fulfillment and freedom. For both Hegelian idealism and Marxian dialectical materialism, the dialectical pattern eventuated in a final culmination which comprehensively unified all human striving and struggle. In a much
more restricted sense, the experimentalism of Dewey, which
Counts embraced, pointed to a stage of human development
in which a comprehensive sharing of man's social and intellectual possessions might possibly occur. This comprehensive sharing would be an on-going and continuing process and would
never reach a final stage as long as human life continued. At
first glance, some tenuous comparisons might be made between
the Marxian and Countian views in the area of the achievement of a comprehensive social organization. This area might
be considered from the point of view of: one, both as reactions
against laissez faire economic individualism; two, the differences between the two positions in terms of determinism.

Both Marx and Counts rejected the classical liberal or laissez
faire philosophy which rested upon the complete individualism
of each person as an independent and atomistic social being.
According to this view, individual needs and interests were prior

to and superior to social needs and interests. To Marx, class interests were prior to and determined individual interests. For Counts, society was based on the association of human beings in group life. As with Dewey, common sharing of things and instruments produced communication and a sense of community between persons involved in associative life. Counts believed that the individual gained freedom only as he accepted the patterns and practices of a particular society. Human freedom and liberty were proportionate to the involvement of the individual in the life of the group. Therefore, both Marx and Counts rejected the theory of social atomism. While Marx emphasized the economic class as the essential social unit, Counts emphasized the cultural group. Both emphasized a more comprehensive social unity than that of the individual.

Although both emphasized a comprehensive social unity, a sharp difference existed between the Marxian and the Countian view. For the Marxist, the most complete and comprehensive life was that which was realized in the highest level of the process of dialectical materialism, the classless society. For Counts, the comprehensive organization of human life was not related to the deterministic dialectical processes. Further, the comprehensive organization of human life was a continuing and on-going process which knew no fixed or determined ends. Through the experimental process, social and institutional life became increasingly interrelated and interconnected. As man, individually and collectively, realized his purposes in action through experimental means, an ever increasing network of human experience was built.

Clearly, Counts's critique of laissez faire economic theory indicated his rejection of social atomism. For him, the greater the degree of cooperation, sharing, and social organization, the greater the degree of human freedom. His educational program as well as his social interpretation stressed the interrelated, co-operative, complex, and socially oriented view of life. To Counts, the rational and intelligent sharing in the common, collective democracy embodied the greatest good because it allowed the greatest possibilities for the growth of human personality. While Counts rejected the closed, deterministic system of dialectical materialism, he advocated the comprehensive and integrated social order which was to result from democratic planning.

Economic Determinism

For Marx, history recorded class conflicts. Economics completely determined social class origin and class struggle. Marxian economic determinism rested on the premise that the means and modes of production constituted the underlying strata or base of the social order. Power in society rested on the control of the economic system, the means and modes of production. Upon this economic foundation or substrata, the institutional superstructure was raised. This legal, political, religious, cultural superstructure was also determined by the economic supporting strata and connected to the relations of production without dependence on human will and action.[3]

In his works of the 1930s, Counts concluded that economics was the conditioning agent in social change. His analysis of the origins of American democracy postulated a pattern of development in which economic equality produced social equality and culminated in political democracy. In his controversy with Bode, Counts concluded that economic reconstruction was basic to other forms of social reconstruction. Counts's predilection to economic conditioning, however, allowed for the operation of human will and preference. Even more essential than economics were the operations of human choice. Although postulating a developmental pattern which relied on economic conditioning, Counts advocated a political program of action designed to reconstruct the economic base, restrict "economic aristocracy," and advance an equalitarian, democratic collectivism. While economic determinism was the sole causal force for Marx, Counts's social theory stressed recognition of the significance of human choice. Since he relied on essentially political measures to restore economic equality, Counts apparently did not believe that human nature was solely an economic product. Throughout this paper, the use of the term "economic determinism" has been studiously avoided in reference to Countian social interpretation. Instead of "economic determinism" the words "economic conditioning" were used to refer to Counts's position during the 1930s. Although "economic conditioning" constituted a very significant element in the theory, this element served as a more restricted causative factor than Marxian "economic determinism." Counts's proposed program of action included in *The Prospects of American Democracy* weakened his earlier economic emphasis. He believed that informed public opinion and concerted political organization and action were capable of reconstructing the economic order.

Class Struggle

According to Marx, social classes resulted from the struggle to control the means and modes of production. Marx found society bipolarly constituted into two rival classes—exploiters and exploited. This class division represented the elements of thesis and antithesis contained within the formula of dialectical materialism. Since the ruling class of exploiters possessed the means and modes of production, this class sought to maintain the status quo in order to perpetuate itself. The exploiting class contained its own antithesis—the exploited class. On the one hand, the exploiting class had to maintain its power basis in the existent property relationships. On the other hand, it sought to expand the power base through technical innovation. Although these innovations increased wealth, they also altered the means and modes of production upon which resided the basis of the class power. As a result of this alteration, a new class arose to threaten the status quo. As the technical conditions of production were changed, the ruling class's accustomed power position also was changed.

The Marxian analysis of the evolution and role of social classes rested upon two premises: the process of dialectical materialism and the factor of economic determinism. As stated earlier, the dialectical process was alien to Counts's social interpretation. However, the economic role was crucial in Counts's social analysis during the 1930s. Although his literary style during the 1930s was colored by the use of class-conscious language, the tendency to use this language seemed to stem from the anticapitalist tendency in American social reform rather than from any reliance on Marxian scientific socialism.

Marx viewed history as the record of class conflict engendered by the operations of the dialectic and the economic evolution. At the first level of this conflict, the primitive communal pattern of simple nomadic life existed. At this primitive level, the antithesis, man, was locked in conflict with the thesis, nature. From this conflict, a new synthesis derived in which the master controlled the means of production through the slave, the antithesis. The third stage was that of the agrarian landlord, thesis, and the middle class, antithesis. At the fourth stage of class evolution, the bourgeoisie thesis, conflicted with the antithesis, the proletariat.

This fourth stage of class conflict was crucial for Marx. Modern society had split into two irreconcilable camps: bourgeois and proletarian. The modern capitalist had fulfilled the revolutionary role by destroying the feudal control of production. Capitalist methods of production brought into existence and then increased the numbers of the exploited class, the proletariat. The capitalist sought to improve production in order to increase profits and simultaneously control productive means. The capitalist's efforts brought about contradictions and also increased the proletarian ranks. By Marxian definition, the proletariat consisted of persons dependent for livelihood on the sale of labor power and unable to earn income except by resigning all claim to the product of their labor to the capitalist.[4] The proletariat survived by laboring upon the machines and materials owned by the capitalists. This Marxian definition embraced the manual workers and ignored the managerial and agricultural workers.

For Marx, the final struggle for control of the means and modes of production was a continuance of the unfolding dialectic, the class war, or the proletarian revolution. In this final struggle, the capitalists were pitted against the proletariat—their economically and dialectically determined successors. It was the unalterable course of history that the proletariat would gain control of the means of production. It was also inevitable that the bourgeoisie would struggle in vain against the sweep of history to retain control of the means and modes of production. The result of the capitalistic attempt to maintain power would result in the violent overthrow of capitalism by the proletarian revolution. In the Marxist analysis of social revolution, only the bourgeoisie and the proletariat had significance.

Groups which could not be immediately classified as belonging to either of the conflicting classes were in reality satellites of these two major groups. They possessed no power to create an alternative social pattern and were allied with one of the major classes.

Although Marxian theory contained limited elements of an evolutionary nature such as technological improvement, it was essentially a theory which rested upon revolution as a means of effecting social change. In contrast, Counts held social change to be evolutionary rather than revolutionary. Instead of viewing history as a conflict between competing classes which progressed through four stages of civilization, Counts believed the evolutionary process had moved through three civilizational stages—hunting, agricultural, and industrial. Like the Marxian interpretation, these three civilizational stages rested on economic arrangements conditioned by a particular geographical and climatic environment. While for Marx, change was unidirectional and unicausal, Counts conceived of the evolutionary process as multidirectional and multicausal. For Counts, social change could result from any number of factors ranging from climatic changes, inventions, and discoveries, to patterns of migration, or even the influence of leading men. For Counts, there were no historical laws which stated that change occurred only through the competition of classes or that a violent revolution was inevitable.

At this point it is necessary to restate that Counts offered no deterministic theory of social change. Rather, he offered a multifactored or multilateral view of social change which can be further clarified by reference to Counts's experimentalist orientation. First, in man's experience with environment, any number of interactive situations might occur. Each of these interactive situations were occasions of social adaptation to environment and, hence, occasions of possible social change. Second, in this process of social adaptation, man did not have to blindly submit to the forces of environment. Rather, through his intelligence, he could harness and transform environmental forces into purposeful instruments. This harnessing of the environment was always conditioned by the specific context of possible materials available in the interactive situation. Since the course of social change was subject only to man's intelligence and the possibilities existent in the particular interactive situation, the experimentalist view precluded adherence to any one set of causal factors or to one determined course of events. While Marx was describing conditions of social change which were universal in application, Counts was concerned with the particular set of conditions which were relevant to the American social order. In the following chapter, "Counts and American Social Reform," Counts's position in American social theory will be discussed. However, even in this particular instance of social change at a given time and place, Counts seemed to offer a social interpretation of the American heritage rather than a well-defined social theory.

During the 1930s, Counts's social and educational analysis was a class-oriented interpretation. He attacked the economic elite which existed at the summit of the American social and economic hierarchy. At the base of the social pyramid rested the mass of society. For Counts, the mass included all those who produced useful goods, services, or ideas. The "economic aristocracy" controlling productive property exploited these contributions of the masses. For Marx, the exploited revolutionary proletariat consisted of the industrial laborers of the world. For Counts, the popular base of industrial society included teachers, scientists, farmers, laborers, and all men engaged in productive activity. While Marx ignored all but the industrial proletariat, Counts considered the mass of society to be more inclusive. While Marx was highly suspicious of the conservative European peasantry, Counts based his interpretation of American democracy upon the agrarian past.

Both Marx and Counts postulated a polarization of society into two major classes: for Marx, the capitalists and the proletariat; for Counts, the "economic aristocracy" and the producing masses. In both cases, this polarization of society ignored the middle rungs of the social ladder. Marx regarded the middle class as a social group which was doomed to be pushed downward into the proletarian ranks. Counts stated that the American middle class imitated slavishly the ideals and aspirations of the economic aristocracy and was unable to provide constructive leadership. Although both Marx and Counts concluded that the emergent civilization would be industrial and technological, both neglected to indicate the role the technicians and the managerial elite would play in the emerging social order. As the experience of both contemporary communist and capitalist nations indicates, the managerial and technical elites have exercised significant roles.

During the 1930s, social theorists such as Stuart Chase, Harold Rugg, and James Burnham indicated that certain intelligent and creative minorities were destined to assume the leadership in the emergent society. Both Chase and Rugg stated that the future lay in the hands of an intelligent minority who would become the locus of rational and comprehensive controls over economic and social life.[5] Burnham discerned that the future would be directed by a class of managers.[6] Counts did not develop any comparable theoretical speculation regarding the development of a ruling elite based upon technological or managerial skills. According to the equalitarian criteria of democracy established by Counts, the minority rule or leadership proposed by Chase, Rugg, and Burnham contained an antiequalitarian and hence antidemocratic tendency. Counts failed to supply an alternative means of ensuring the continuance of equalitarian democratic processes in the light of the inevitable increase in power of the managerial-technical groups in a highly industrialized society. The formula presented by Counts was that of continued reliance on democratic political processes.

Surplus Value

For Marx, wealth in capitalistic societies was measured by the accumulation of commodities. A commodity was an external object that satisfied human need and was exchangeable for other products or commodities. The value of the commodity was determined by the amount of socially necessary labor required to produce it. Thus, labor power for Marx became a commodity. In exchange for his labor, the worker received a wage to sustain him for further productive activities. The value of labor created more exchange value than the product was worth of itself. The result was creation of surplus value which was expropriated by the capitalist.[7]

Counts's social interpretation did not refer to these concepts used by Marx such as "socially necessary labor," or "surplus value." Although he concluded that the "economic aristocracy" expropriated the productive wealth of the nation, Counts did not indicate the precise operations involved in this expropriation. He did predict that in a society controlled by the "economic aristocracy," the producing mass would be allowed only the goods and services necessary to keep them at optimum working capacity. The aristocracy would use the accumulated wealth for their own satisfaction.

Vanguard of the Proletariat

According to Marx, a significant role was exercised by the group of bourgeois ideologists who detached themselves from their economic class and led the proletariat against the exploiters. This vanguard of the proletariat was able to comprehend the course of history which would culminate in the proletarian revolution and the emergence of the classless society. This small group of intellectuals escaped their economically determined class position because they were far removed from the means and modes of production. Included among this vanguard of the proletariat were the sons of the bourgeoisie, Marx and Engels.

It is difficult to find in Counts any group which precisely corresponds to the vanguard of the proletariat. Since Counts allowed greater freedom to individual choice and restricted the causative factors of economic determinism, it was possible for individuals from any class to reconstruct the social order. Indeed, Counts's educational program was designed to facilitate this enlightened analysis which projected the building of a new social order. Certain tenuous comparisons might be made between the vanguard of the proletariat in Marxian theory and the teachers who were to lead in building a new social order in Counts's theory. Although American teachers were mainly from middle class groups, they were to overcome the value orientation associated with the individualism of this class and actively promote the emergence of democratic collectivism.

Counts assumed that teachers were naturally sympathetic to the productive masses and urged them to ally with these classes in the building of a new social order. Despite his attention to class status as a factor in school board membership and secondary school attendance, Counts did not investigate the class origins of American teachers. Rather, he felt that the education of teachers and their predilection to the scientific method would enable them to seek and intelligently use power to build a new social order.

Marxian Revolution

According to Marx, capitalism incurred its own destruction by ruthless profit-seeking and overproduction which culminated in crises, slumps, and depressions. Unable to coordinate productivity, capitalism was compelled to reinvest capital to increase production without guarantees of consumption of the commodities produced. The misery of recurrent economic depressions caused increasing discontent among members of the chronically unemployed proletariat. Under these oppressive conditions, the proletariat was destined to revolt, throw off the shackles of an oppressive capitalism, and seize control of the means and modes of production. This proletarian revolution would then establish a dictatorship which centralized all productive instruments, increased total productive capacity, and initiated reforms leading to a classless society. With the classless society, the dialectical process was fulfilled and ceased its movement. Although Marx believed that violent revolution might be unnecessary in advanced Western nations, the usual pattern of inaugurating the dictatorship of the proletariat occurred through violent class warfare.

During the 1930s, Counts was extremely critical of capitalism which he accused of bringing about the depression. In a highly organized, cooperative, technological society, Counts felt that capitalism based on economic individualism and the profit motive was obsolete. The immediate problems of economic depression and increasingly high unemployment caused him to reject capitalism and to propose a system of democratic collectivism. Despite his verbal attacks on capitalism, Counts believed it possible to avoid class warfare in the United States through the means of enlightened and concerted political action. He continued to place faith in the democratic methodology of discussion, debate, and decision through parliamentary procedure and majority rule. He rejected the Marxian advocacy of social change through violent revolution. He believed that peaceful social change was possible through the use of critical intelligence, scientific method, and the democratic processes. Further, the conspiratorial means of subversion advocated by Marx were anathema to the open-ended method and practice urged by Counts. He rejected dictatorships of any kind since the favored class, even a working class, would exercise dictatorial power and militate against further change. Marx's predicted classless society constituted a predetermined end which was precluded by Counts's instrumentalism. Thus, Counts did not indicate precisely the exact contours and forms which the emergent collective democracy would assume. The precise patterns of collective democracy were to be fashioned by the creative intelligence and experimentation of the American people.

Despite his desire to minimize violence as a means of securing social change, Counts did not completely rule out armed revolution. Violent class warfare was to be only a last resort for an oppressed people. He believed that the political means of redress and of change were still adequate to secure genuine political, economic, and social democracy. However, if further concentration of wealth and consequently of power gravitated to the upper economic class so that the political processes became inoperative, then the popular masses were justified in resorting to force to redress their grievances.

Marxism and the State

After achieving the classless society, Marx stated that the now obsolete state would wither away in the new revolutionary society. To Marx, the state was a repressive instrument used by the exploiting class to control the exploited. Counts held no illusion about any such withering away of the state. For him, the state was a neutral and necessary instrument. As a neutral instrument, it could serve either majority or minority interests. In the American political tradition, the state was a political institution which functioned to serve majoritarian interests and also safeguard essential civil rights. As an instrumental and political reality, Counts believed the state could be ordered and reconstructed to meet changing conditions and needs.

Marxian theory was supranational and maintained that the international proletariat belonged to the same class and was not to be misled by the artificially contrived capitalist sentiment of loyalty to the national state. This loyalty or patriotism to nation rather than to class alienated the proletariat from their true interests. Counts, in contrast, believed that every society had a peculiar heritage and tradition. As stated many times, education was conditioned by the needs and patterns of a particular society at a particular time and place. In accepting the existence of the national state system, Counts stated that in the forseeable future man's life would be patterned by allegiance to the national state.

During the 1930s, Counts indicated that international rivalries and conflicts were caused to a large degree by economic rivalries. However, the menacing rise of the totalitarian states in the late 1930s led him away from placing large significance on the role of economic conflict in producing international conflict.

Although Counts emphasized class differences during the depression period, the total cultural patterns of a particular civilization seemed to be more of a formative force than membership in a particular economic class. Counts was convinced that man was nurtured by a particular culture and gained freedom by completely identifying himself with the particular cultural heritage. While Marx postulated a universal social philosophy, Counts fashioned a social theory that partook of the American cultural heritage and was restricted to that heritage.

The importance of socio-economic class was one of Counts's major concerns in his analysis of American society. His early works on the secondary school and the social composition of boards of education referred to the class basis of both students and board members. This class basis was occupationally determined, which was an evidence of economic conditioning. Although economic class was divisive and led to the formation of an economic elite which dominated society, Counts believed that the divisive tendency of rigid economic class could be overcome. First, a devotion and loyalty to the democratic heritage could act as a unifying force and could also lead to the emergent collectivism. Secondly, positive attempts could be undertaken to limit the great economic gap which had developed between classes. Although Counts emphasized class during the 1930s, his later writings gave greater emphasis to the common, democratic, American heritage.

Comparison of Marx and Counts

In conclusion, certain similarities exist between Marxian and Countian theory. First, both theories placed emphasis on the motive force of economics. However, this similarity must be qualified since Marxian theory was deterministic while Counts allowed for the operations of human choice. Second, both theories emphasized class. For Counts, class was subordinate to the total cultural pattern. Finally, Marxian theory and Countian theory varied widely on philosophical and methodological bases. Dialectical materialism was alien to the open-endedness of instrumentalism adhered to by Counts. While Marx relied primarily on class warfare and revolution, Counts allowed for wide areas of peaceful, evolutionary change. The conspiratorial, violent advocacy of class warfare differed vastly from Counts's reliance on reasoned democracy and parliamentary processes. Marxian dictatorship of the proletariat meant rule by elite for Counts. Marxian classless society and the withering away of the state were vastly different from Counts's democratic collectivism which took no definite, predetermined form.

Why then was Counts so frequently associated with Marxism during the 1930s? To the superficial observer, Counts's interest in a planned and collectivistic economic system may have seemed a form of scientific Marxism. The interest in the Soviet experiment of economic planning may have indicated a preference for Marxism. Throughout this book, it has been pointed out that Counts rejected the Soviet methods despite his interest in the Soviet achievements during the period of the Five Year Plans. His struggle against communist infiltration into the American Federation of Teachers has also been mentioned.

Perhaps, the Countian terminology may have caused some of the more superficial readers of Counts's works to conclude that he was a Marxist. Such words as "collectivism," "class struggle," and "economic aristocracy" undoubtedly conjured fears of the coming revolution in the minds of his readers. Even the mention of the word "imposition" may have raised fears in the minds of some educators. Despite the ominous sounding phraseology, Counts relied on the democratic methods and processes and rejected totalitarianism of both political left and right. Although these tenuous similarities between Marxism and Counts's theory have been pointed out, it is necessary to go to the American cultural tradition of social reformism to more accurately trace the roots of his social and educational theories.

1. Lawrence A. Cremin, *The Transformation of the School* (New York: Alfred A. Knopf, 1962), p. 259.

2. Harold L. Varney, "Class-War on the Campus," *American Mercury*, 40 (1937), 465.

3. John Plamenttz, *German Marxism and Russian Communism* (New York: Longmans, Green & Co., 1954), p. 24.

4. G. D. H. Cole, *What Marx Really Meant?* (New York: Alfred A. Knopf, 1937), p. 102.

5. Stuart Chase, *A New Deal* (New York: Macmillan Co., 1932); Harold Rugg, *The Great Technology* (New York: John Day Co., 1933).

6. James Burnham, *The Managerial Revolution* (New York: John Day Co., 1941).

7. Sidney Hook, *Towards the Understanding of Karl Marx* (London: Victor Gallancz, 1933), p. 172.

X. Counts and American Social Reform

Although certain tenuous comparisons can be made between Marxian theory and the theory of George S. Counts, the origins of Counts's theory rested within the framework of the American tradition of social reform and protest. To locate Counts's theoretical position on the grid of American experience, three main currents of social and political theory can be differentiated. First, there is the theoretical position associated with political and social conservatism. Clustered about this conservative position are such subsidiary movements as Hamiltonian Federalism, economic individualism, Social Darwinism, industrial capitalism, and traditional laissez faire classical liberalism. The second major position of social and political theory in the American tradition has reflected opposition to the ideas and practices contained within this conservative movement. In protest against big business domination, currents of popular democracy have clustered around such movements as Jeffersonian agrarianism, Jacksonian democracy, pragmatism, progressivism, and the New Deal. This second current has been designated as the "new liberalism" in contrast to the older form of classical liberalism. Although the "new liberalism" has demonstrated a propensity for encouraging social reform, the means of effecting this reform have been usually evolutionary, peaceful, and gradual.

In addition to conservatism and liberalism, there has existed a third theoretical posture in American social and political theory, which has often served as a focus of social protest and discontent. This third area contained social views that can be loosely designated as sometimes idealistic, sometimes utopian, and at other times radically revolutionary. Within this third current have been found such movements as American socialism and populism, and such personalities as Eugene V. Debs, Henry George, and Edward Bellamy. Although never in a position of actual power, this third current of social protest has exercised a marked influence on the American scene. While it has sometimes furnished design and inspiration to the new liberalism, it has also produced fears among the conservatives which often culminated in periods of social reaction.

American educational theory has often been associated with major political movements. Merle Curti associated Henry Barnard and William T. Harris with the capitalistic and conservatively oriented classical liberalism. Lawrence Cremin has attempted to relate progressive education to political progressivism. During the 1930s, Counts seems to have occupied a position which existed somewhat between the mainsprings of American evolutionary liberalism characterized by the New Deal of Franklin Roosevelt and the heritage of social protest and radical discontent. Counts's analysis of the American social order during the 1930s resembled that of the more radical social theorists. However, his solutions to the problems of the depression were much more moderate and took a form of political action which resembled the gradualistic reformism of the New Deal. At times, Counts formulated an educational philosophy and program which corresponded to the political philosophy and program of the New Deal. At other times, he veered to the left of the New Deal and embraced more of the orientation of radical social protest and discontent.

To more adequately define Counts's position in the currents of American life, it is necessary to explore briefly the heritage which contributed to his social and educational theory. Much of this heritage was the common sharing of the progressive tradition in American political and educational theory. Within the theory of Counts can be found elements of evolutionary naturalism, the American frontier tradition, pragmatic instrumentalism, political reformism, utopianism, the "new history," and the depression oriented milieu of the 1930s.

Evolutionary Naturalism

Although by the time of Counts's emergence as an educational theorist the Darwinian revolution was well on its course, he, like Dewey and others, was influenced by the tenets of an evolutionary naturalism. Unlike some of his contemporaries, Counts was little troubled by the impact of Darwinism upon his earlier attitudes. In his secondary classes in rural Kansas shortly after the turn of the century, Counts taught the theory of evolution. John Childs in *American Pragmatism and Education* wrote that Counts thought of man and society in evolutionary and functional terms. He conceived of human behavior as the product of interaction between man and environment. Learning was a function of this adaptive process, and man was a creator and a creature of culture.[1]

The Darwinian theory of evolution held that change was the basic characteristic of life in the world. The physical universe, geography, and geology exhibited a long history of change and development. The American experience, conditioned by changing agricultural and industrial frontiers, welcomed the rationale provided by Darwinism and its interpreters. As a youth in rural Kansas, Counts witnessed men at work changing the natural environment and adapting it to patterns of control. In turn, patterns of human life were transformed by the changed environment. The westward advancing frontiersman constantly came into contact with varying sets of environmental conditions. His adaptation to this mosaic environmental pattern built up the legacy of the frontier experience which has long since influenced American historians and social theorists. As the frontiersman struggled to tame the wilderness, a condition of constant flux and changing social patterns characterized his interaction with the natural environment. Man proved to be adaptive to these changing modes of life and developed a social philosophy conducive to the facilitation of still further change. As the agricultural frontier moved progressively westward, the older northern and eastern areas of the United States, too, experienced change wrought by an expansive industrialism.

For American intellectual life, the Darwinian revolution produced great ferment. Traditional modes of religious, social, economic, and political belief were subjected to anguished questioning and reappraisal. Theories of philosophy, psychology, and education were subjected to critical analysis and reconstruction. In the main, two opposing groups of social theorists emerged from the intellectual revolution wrought by Darwinism.

Social Darwinism, allied with the conservative social and

political orientation, used the new theory of biological Darwinism to rationalize the ruthless competition and rugged individualism which characterized American capitalism. In particular, William G. Sumner held that the process of evolutionary change had occurred over long periods of time. As life conditions changed, only then did man's folkways and mores also change. Man could not deliberately interfere with this gradual process of change. Rather, man had to adjust to changing life conditions in order to survive. Successful modes of adjustment were crystalized and ritualized in a set of folkways and mores produced by man's successful trial-and-error adjustment. This interpretation provided a convenient rationale for the "captains of industry" who were carving large industrial and financial empires in the developing American industrial revolution. It was accepted also by political and social leaders who believed in laissez faire and economic individualism. Militating against the proponents of directed and deliberate social change, Social Darwinism urged the passive acceptance of the status quo.

In contrast to the theorists who defended the status quo, others such as Lester F. Ward, George H. Mead, and John Dewey derived from the Darwinian revolution a belief that change could be rationally and deliberately directed by man.[2] Through careful and scientific planning, man could alter his environment to his purposes and needs. Using the scientific method as an instrument to control and direct change, man could harness natural forces as he had once tamed the frontier wilderness into an hospitable environment. This strain of evolutionary naturalism fitted the reforming spirit of the progressive movement in American political history. It was also accepted by progressive educators who attempted to reform American educational theory and practice. Through the pioneering work of John Dewey, this instrumentalist evolutionary naturalism produced ramifications in American jurisprudence, social life, political life, and education. It was this strain of evolutionary naturalism which influenced the work of George S. Counts during the 1930s.

Like Dewey, Counts held that human life was the story of man's interaction with environment. As he successfully harnessed environment, man learned through trial and error processes. Not solely restricted to merely adjusting to environmental conditions, the funded knowledge of man, his past experience, could be harnessed and utilized to transform both the natural and man-made environment. The modern environment of industrialization and technology was created by man and could therefore be ordered into a rationally organized, collectively controlled, and balanced social environment.

Through centuries of trial and error, the man-made environment has developed into a vast industrial complex. As Counts viewed life in the depression-ridden 1930s, this industrial complex could remain a jungle of ruthless competition for survival or it could be ordered into an efficient society of plenty for all through cooperative planning and sharing. Counts's entire thesis rested on the social faith that man could control his destiny through the rational and deliberate means of directing social change to lead to the society of democratic collectivism. His projected democratic collectivism was a form of social engineering through which Americans could control the industrial and technological complex of modern society. Education was to be one of the means which would aid in the construction of this new social order by giving man theory and practice with the instruments of control. Through the instruments of democracy and technology, Counts believed that man could control and harness environment for social welfare.

In discussing the influence of evolutionary naturalism upon Counts, no attempt has been made to place him in the role of a germinal thinker in regard to the evolutionary implications for a planned society. Rather than an innovator in this area, Counts channelled the currents of a reformed Darwinism as derived from Dewey and used them to fashion a projection of the society of the future. He did not attempt to formulate any universal scheme for interpreting social change, nor did he conceive of a world society. Rather, he restricted his interpretation to the limited milieu of the American experience. He attempted to interpret this particular experience in historical-sociological terms which utilized the newly emerged social sciences. He hoped this interpretation would be used by American educators in the building of a new society upon the democratic framework of the old order. An evolutionary naturalism contributed to his arguments for gradual and peaceful social change.

The New History

Counts's projected democratic collectivism was based on a particular interpretation of the American heritage known as the "new history." The historical profession was affected by the rise of pragmatism conditioned by Darwinism, by Dewey's instrumentalism, and by the reformed jurisprudence of Oliver Wendell Holmes, Jr.[3] The pragmatic spirit so evident in the era of progressivism in American political life was reflected in the pragmatic relativism of historical interpretation. American historians such as Carl L. Becker and Charles A. Beard, influenced by pragmatic philosophy, were infused with the freedom of the secular spirit—a belief in the relevance of time and circumstance to truth and value. They shared a common confidence in the practical, the technological, and an involvement with modern social problems.[4]

The "new history" of Becker and Beard saw the reconstruction of the past as a temporary appraisal based on the historian's values and tempered by his particular time, circumstances, and personality. Historical reconstruction was conceived as the record of the functional adjustment of an organism to environment to satisfy the needs arising from a particular situational experience.[5] The view of the past became a projection of the ideas and interests of the present upon the accumulated data of remembered or recorded experience.[6] According to the new history, the historian was to operate in the realm of value as well as of fact. The historian was to recognize and utilize his values to reconstruct history and place historical research in the area of contemporary social problems. The new history represented a challenge to the allegedly value-free history or "scientific history" of the von Ranke school. In contrast to objectivism in historical writing, Becker, for example, believed that man's experience, purpose, interest, and value were the proper areas of historical research.[7]

Counts's close association with Charles A. Beard as a personal friend and as a member of the Commission of the American Historical Association on the Social Studies in the Schools brought him into acquaintance with one of the major proponents of the new history. Counts's own interpretation of the American heritage seemed to rely on the economic interpretation offered by Beard. Counts stressed the relativism embodied in the new history and argued for cultural and educational relativism. Robert E. Mason in *Educational Ideas in American Society* stated that the new history profoundly affected educational theory as it shifted from conventional, systematic history to emphasis on social problems. History was no longer conceived of as a purely objective and impartial discipline but rather as an instrument to render principles for guiding human effort in the reconstruction of the contemporary social order.[8] Counts used as the basis for his conception of democracy a particular interpretation of American history. His educational theory also flowed from this interpretation which was permeated with an economic view. Thus the factor of economic conditioning assumed a significance of major importance in Counts's writings during the 1930s.

Counts claimed that he was especially indebted to the historical researches of Charles A. Beard. In the *Economic Origins of Jeffersonian Democracy* and *The Economic Basis of Politics,* as well as other works, Beard had used an economic interpretation of history. He discussed the economic group interests of the various sectors of the American public as the very essence of political life.[9] Like Counts, Beard also stressed the freehold period of agrarian economic equality as the foundational period of American democracy. According to Beard, the Jeffersonian period with its wide distribution of land ownership brought about a considerable amount of economic equality from which flowed political and social equality.[10]

Like Counts, Beard also had pointed to John Taylor of Caroline, who attacked the Federalist sympathizers of Hamilton, as an early example of an exponent of American equalitarianism. Taylor alleged that a new class, capitalistic in character, had sprung up, based on exploitation through inflated public paper, bank stock, and the protective tariff. According to Taylor, a fundamental conflict between capitalistic and agrarian interests served as the point of origin of American political parties.[11] Thus Beard used Taylor's arguments to indicate the origin of American political parties on the basis of economic class. Counts also used Taylor's definition of minority to describe the composition of the economic aristocracy and to condemn the ascendancy of this minority group over American life in the 1930s. He also pointed to Taylor as a representative figure in the struggle between economic classes during the earlier American republican period.

During the depression of the 1930s, Beard also argued for social and economic planning and was a frequent contributor to *Social Frontier,* edited by Counts. In *Toward Civilization* (1930) Beard stated that an inherited agricultural mentality was blocking the formulation of an ethical system suited to an engineering age. He wrote that it was possible to achieve a new civilization with ethical potentialities inconceivable under an economy of perilous and marginal life. Within the scientific method, he concluded, lay the possibilities of both plan and control.[12] Counts quoted Beard's analysis of the diffusion of engineering rationality into industry, business, government, and social life in *The Social Foundations of Education.* Beard alleged that the diffusion of technical rationality was founded on an economic base and intimately involved in the operations of a productive economy.[13] In *America in Midpassage* (1939) Beard cited Counts: "George S. Counts of the Teachers' College at Columbia University drew up in 1938 an impressive balance sheet of assets and liabilities in *The Prospects of American Democracy,* laid down a program for constructive action, and issued a call for a concert of popular powers in America." [14]

In creating a frame of reference for his educational theory, Counts used an interpretation of American history which rested on the interpretation of the new history, especially the economic interpretation of Beard. It made no attempt at historical objectivism but rather offered a specific interpretation

of American history conceived in terms of the frontier experience and the legacy of cooperative activities. Such an interpretation of the American heritage was not history for the sake
of academic exercise, but it was rather conceived as an instru-
mentality for use in the solution of social, political, and economic problems of the contemporary period. By revealing the
conflict areas which required solutions, the new history was
used as a guide to the past to direct present inquiry and to
shape future activity.

In formulating a philosophy of education for a collectivistic
age, Counts derived his educational theory from a particular
tradition in American history. He used the agrarian, populist,
progressive, social reformist tradition and attempted to relate
this tradition to what he conceived to be the emergent realities
of American society: technology and democracy. Counts seized
upon the Jeffersonian equalitarian aspects of the heritage of a
frontier-agrarian economy as a foundation for the emergent
democratic-collectivist economy and society. For long periods
of history, this reformist tradition had been submerged by the
ascendancy of the capitalistic, laissez faire, economic individualistic tradition which Counts referred to as the Hamiltonian
tradition. Since collectivistic society could follow either pattern, Jeffersonian or Hamiltonian, democratic or aristocratic,
Counts emphasized the Jeffersonian heritage as a means of
directing a popular, equalitarian, democratic social reconstructionism.

Mason stated that some form of indoctrination was inescapable in educational work as it was in the writing of history. The new historians used a frame of reference in writing
history as did the progressive educational theorists in creating
a new formula for American educational philosophy and practice.[15] Thus, it was of extreme importance to decide deliber-

ately and critically which point of view was to dominate educational effort. Counts during the 1930s deliberately sought to persuade the educational profession to express a commitment on behalf of the equalitarian-Jeffersonian tradition and on behalf of the democratic-collectivistic future. This theme recurred throughout Counts's works, especially in *The Social Foundations of Education* and *The Prospects of American Democracy*. The plea for an education committed to a form of collective democracy also permeated the works of the Commission of the American Historical Association on the Social Studies in the Schools. Counts's reliance on the new relativistic history marked a significant influence in the development of his interpretation of the American heritage and in his framing of an educational theory.

Utopian Reformism: George and Bellamy

Counts's works, especially *The Prospects of American Democracy*, were works of social protest and discontent as well as of educational theory. As already mentioned, Counts discussed the rise of an economic aristocracy which menaced the equalitarian and democratic foundations of popular government in the United States. Part of Counts's critique of American industrial capitalism resembled the earlier manifestations of social discontent and protest which occurred in the United States at the close of the nineteenth century. *A Call to the Teachers of the Nation* (1933) called attention to the writings of Henry George and Edward Bellamy. Theodore Brameld's *Toward a Reconstructed Philosophy of Education* indicated that there were some connections between educational reconstructionism and the earlier social and political reconstructionists such as Bellamy and George. Brameld said that, although Counts had modified his position in recent years, he still had strong utopian tendencies and harbored an increased appreciation of the genuine democratic tradition. Further, according to Brameld, although Counts made initial contributions to reconstructionism in his *Dare the School Build a New Social Order?*, he remained essentially a progressive whose views could be both lauded and criticized in terms of the strengths and weaknesses of a general philosophic orientation.[16]

Henry George's *Progress and Poverty* was a severe indictment against the capitalistic system based upon observations during the 1860s and 1870s. George challenged the prevailing theories of laissez faire liberalism in economics and Social Darwinism in sociology and politics. George asked why so much misery and poverty existed in an age of science and technology? Why did these conditions of privation continue when inventions and machines were capable of creating wealth and well-being? He believed that the cause of economic inequality lay in inadequate social organization and particularly in the prevailing system of land ownership. He oversimplified the economic problems of the growing industrial order by urging a single tax on land which he believed would benefit the whole of society.[17] Despite the oversimplification of his economic theory, George's works of social protest attracted great attention at the turn of the century and constituted a theoretical argument for social and economic reform.

In 1888, Edward Bellamy wrote *Looking Backward*, a novel of social protest and a scheme for the nationalization of industry under the leadership of a national industrial army. Bellamy's work attracted and influenced the thought of men like John Dewey, Eugene V. Debs, Norman Thomas, and Charles A. Beard.[18] The gist of Bellamy's work was that industrial development was moving to greater and greater consolidation and centralization in the United States. He viewed the cartels, trusts, and monopolies of industrial capitalism as only a step along the road to the complete consolidation of industrial life which would be eventually effected by the national army. Under the national industrial army, economic control would be rational, efficient, and democratic.[19] In criticism of his world of 1888, Bellamy singled out the waste, inefficiency, and privation which resulted from unchecked competition and from the periodical gluts and economic crises associated with modern capitalism.[20]

Although it would constitute an unwarranted generalization to state that Counts was directly influenced by the utopian critics of industrial capitalism, his works indicate that he was familiar with and sympathetic to these early social protests of George and Bellamy. Although Counts claimed to be completely realistic in his social theory, certain elements of the utopianism of the late nineteenth-century American movement of social protest are apparent in his works. He seemed to combine two basic emphases in his social theory: a descriptive and a futuristic emphasis. Counts's works were descriptive as they reflected the interpretations of the "new history." The treatment of the agrarian origins, the growth of industrial capitalism, and the excesses of economic individualism constituted a large part of the descriptive portions of his work. After the descriptive or expository materials were presented, Counts projected a very generalized view of the society of the future— the society of democratic collectivism. In his projected view of the new social order, he presented what might be termed a faith and a vision in a democratic vista of the future based upon his particular conception of the American heritage. Outside of urging informed and organized political action and an educational program committed to democratic collectivism, Counts failed to clearly indicate a program of action to achieve this vision. Although the exposition of the American past, the criticisms of the American present, and the view of the American future were inspiring, neither a clearly defined program of immediate action nor a set of precise analytical concepts and instruments emerged to guide the building of a new social order along lines of democratic collectivism. In this sense Counts reflected the utopian social reformers of the past. This is not to say that Counts was essentially utopian in the 1930s but rather that this element was present in his writings during the depression period.

Further, like many utopians, Counts's theory hearkened back to a golden age in the past. He returned for his ideals to what was in some respects the great period of relative equality of economic, social, and political life during the freehold period in American history. From this historic era were derived many of the ideals and aspirations of the future envisioned by Counts. Although the equality of condition of the freehold democracy may have been partially true, a large degree of economic, social, and even political disparity existed. In pointing to the protests of Jefferson and Taylor against the monied classes, Beard and Counts provided evidence of this disparity in the age to which they returned for inspiration.

Thus, at times, Counts veered from the path of evolutionary reformism characterized by the New Deal. He entered the area of heightened social protest and discontent which had once characterized the American utopian reformers of the late 1880s and 1890s. But perhaps even more significant than this element of social protest was the very period in which Counts developed his theory of democratic-collectivism, the period of the great depression of the 1930s.

Influence of the Depression Milieu

Counts's educational and social theories during the 1930s reflected the depression period. He admittedly operated on the theoretical premise that education was conditioned by a particular civilization at a particular time and place. In the light of his own operational criteria, it can be stated that Counts's educational and social theory represented the currents of the social, economic, and political milieu of the 1930s. Counts, and most of the progressive, socially oriented educators, accepted the tenets of political progressivism and liberal democracy which were expressed in the progressive movement of the early twentieth century and in the New Deal of the 1930s. Mason's critique of educational pragmatism in *Educational Ideals in American Society* found that educational pragmatism was closely related to political and economic liberalism in the years between the two world wars. He termed these liberals "quantitative liberals" who were concerned with immediate problems of economic subsistence and survival.[21] Cremin has also associated educational progressivism and political progressivism.

Counts was generally sympathetic to the New Deal legislation of President Franklin Roosevelt. He believed that the New Deal period may have been the threshold to the era of democratic collectivism. Although the *Social Frontier* was usually sympathetic to the New Deal experimentation and legislation, it contained a note which was critical. Many of the journal's contributors felt that Roosevelt's administration lacked a consistent and comprehensive program for social, economic, and political reform. Beyond this criticism, Counts's *The So-*

cial Foundations of Education and *The Prospects of American Democracy* generally supported the Roosevelt program against the opposition of the Supreme Court and the American Liberty League. In addition to this sympathy for direct political action and activity, certain theoretical works associated with the depression period seemed to have had an influence on Counts's ideas during the 1930s.

In *The Prospects of American Democracy* (1938) Counts cited the well-known economic study of Berle and Means, *The Modern Corporation and Private Property* (1932). He used their statistics as evidence to illustrate the tendency for the concentration of wealth into the hands of the aristocracy and to support his criticism of the increasing class stratification of American society on economic lines. Berle and Means made an exhaustive study of the modern American corporate structure. Although they indicated that wealth was being concentrated, they also drew several other conclusions which Counts seemed to have neglected in his works during the 1930s. One of their most significant analyses pointed to the separation of ownership from control. While the owner of industrial wealth retained a symbol of ownership in the form of stock, the power, responsibility, and substance of this ownership was transferred to a separate group which exercised the actual control and power.[22] Berle and Means also pointed to a tendency for the dispersion of stock ownership. Although this dispersion had reached a point where no one individual owned a major part of the stock, the authors stated that this trend appeared to be gaining momentum and required further study. They also pointed to the rise of what might be a purely neutral technocracy of administrators and managers who, while not owners, exercised control over economic, productive, and industrial wealth.[23]

Although Counts accepted the conclusions of Berle and Means regarding the demise of economic individualism and the institutionalization of the corporate structure, he failed to elaborate these other tendencies regarding modern industrial capitalism in his interpretation. While Berle and Means pointed to the complexities involved in the rising corporate structure, Counts's criticisms of the "economic aristocracy" and the concentration of productive property oversimplified the analysis of the corporate structure. Certainly, all agreed that the corporation was a part of the emerging technological and industrial social order. However, instead of dealing with these impersonal forces, Counts focused his criticism against unnamed persons who were responsible for the concentration of productive property. His attack on the privileged class resembled the older agrarian and populist critiques of capitalism instead of analyzing the implications of the tendency to separation of ownership and control. Counts's oversimplification of the problems of the modern corporation alleged that certain groups had sinister motives in gaining power as an outgrowth of their economic position.

Stuart Chase's many books during the depression period also contained a critique of modern capitalism. Chase, like Counts, discussed a lag between production and distribution. He said that contemporary economic thinking reflected the period of economic scarcity. Chase further criticized the profit motive and the residues of laissez faire economic theory which persisted in modern economic thought. He pointed, too, to the need for cooperative activity and social planning.[24] Unlike Counts, Chase suggested a collectivism in which control came from the higher echelons of the technological elite. He urged a national planning board controlled by the federal government and manned by engineers, physical scientists, statisticians, economists, accountants, and lawyers. In addition, representatives of industry, finance, labor, and agriculture were to be added to the projected national planning board to preserve the formal appearance of democracy. The real impetus for collectivism, according to Chase, was to come from an "intelligent minority" organized in every community of the nation under a national coordinating body. This minority which Chase styled the "scientificos" was to lead the nation to collectivism.[25] James Burnham in *The Managerial Revolution* spoke of an elite of managers who would govern the new society. Burnham felt that western civilization was in a period of transition characterized by a rapid rate of change in the economic, social, political, and cultural institutions of society. The general plane of transition was from a capitalistic to a managerial society.[26] Harold Rugg, another educator, spoke of an "intelligent minority" of approximately 25,000,000 persons which was to lead the nation to the age of the new technology.[27]

Although theorists such as Burnham, Chase, and Rugg speculated about the emergence of a planning elite, a managerial class, or an enlightened minority, Counts seemed to have ignored the problems which the rise of the class of managers or experts would bring to the task of creating a collectivistic, technological society within the contours of a democratic framework. The rise of such an elite would have blocked the equalitarian basis which Counts held necessary for democracy unless certain safeguards were postulated. It would seem that such an elite group would naturally result from the growth of a technological society and of a planned and managed economy. Instead of exploring the consequences which the rise of such an elite class or the separation of ownership and management of property for the democratic political structure would have, Counts laid the problems at the door of an ill-defined "economic aristocracy." Apparently this reference to an "economic aristocracy" referred to a class of wealthy individuals rather than to the aggregation of property into corporate and impersonal control to which Berle and Means referred.

The general frame of reference to Counts's works appeared to rest in the soil of native American political liberalism and social protest rather than in the climate of European scientific socialism. Within this tradition, the elements of evolutionary naturalism, pragmatic instrumentalism, the new history, utopian reformism, and the milieu of the depression period represented the various streams of American thought which were evident in the social and educational theory of George S. Counts.

1. John L. Childs, *American Pragmatism and Education* (New York: Henry Holt & Co., 1956), p. 214.

2. The notion of a two-tracked and contrasting Darwinian revolution in social and political theory can be found in Richard Hofstadter, *Social Darwinism in American Thought* (Boston: Beacon Press, 1958), and in R. Freeman Butts and Lawrence A. Cremin, *A History of Education in American Culture* (New York: Holt, Rinehart & Winston, 1953). According to this interpretation, the Darwinian biological theory had implications that were elaborated by such Social Darwinists as Spencer and Sumner into a defense for a competitive and highly individualistic society. However, such "reformed Darwinists" as Ward, Mead, and Dewey used Darwinism as a theoretical support for a cooperative society.

3. Lloyd R. Sorenson, "Charles A. Beard and German Historical Thought," *Mississippi Valley Historical Review*, 42 (1953), 275.

4. Cushing Strout, *The Pragmatic Revolt in American History: Carl Becker and Charles Beard* (New Haven, Conn.: Yale University Press, 1958), p. 7.

5. Ibid.

6. Conyers Read, "The Social Responsibilities of the Historian," *American Historical Review*, 55 (1950), 280.

7. Carl L. Becker, _Progress and Power_ (Stanford: Stanford University Press, 1935), p. 14.

8. Robert E. Mason, _Educational Ideas in American Society_ (Boston: Allyn & Bacon Co., 1960), p. 81.

9. Charles A. Beard, _The Economic Basis of Politics_ (New York: Alfred A. Knopf, 1934), p. 67.

10. Ibid., p. 83.

11. Charles A. Beard, _Economic Origins of Jeffersonian Democracy_ (New York: Macmillan Co., 1927), pp. 351–52.

12. _Toward Civilization_, ed. Charles A. Beard (New York: Longmans, Green & Co., 1930), p. 303.

13. Ibid., p. 301.

14. Charles and Mary Beard, _America in Midpassage_ (New York: Macmillan Co., 1939), pp. 921–22.

15. Mason, _Educational Ideas_, pp. 104–5.

16. Theodore Brameld, _Toward a Reconstructed Philosophy of Education_ (New York: Dryden Press, 1956), p. 160.

17. Saul K. Padover, _The Genius of America_ (New York: McGraw-Hill Book Co., 1960), pp. 227–28.

18. Erich Fromm, in Edward Bellamy, _Looking Backward_ (New York: New American Library, 1960), p. v.

19. Ibid., p. 53.

20. Ibid., p. 157.

21. Mason, _Educational Ideals_, p. 276.

22. Berle and Means, _The Modern Corporation and Private Property_ (New York: Commerce Clearing House, 1932), p. 68.

23. Ibid., p. 356.

24. Stuart Chase, _A New Deal_ (New York: Macmillan Co., 1932), pp. 1–2.

25. Ibid., pp. 248–49.

26. James Burnham, _The Managerial Revolution_ (New York: John Day Co., 1941), pp. 71–72.

27. Harold Rugg, _The Great Technology_ (New York: John Day Co., 1933), pp. 24–25.

XI. Counts's Educational Position

Counts was trained in the scientific aspects of education under Charles Judd at the University of Chicago. While he received his doctorate in education, he did an equal amount of
work in sociology under Albion W. Small. His training in sociology was significant in that this experience introduced him
to the ferment produced by Darwinism in the intellectual
sphere and also to the formal theories of Sumner and Marx.
This early educational experience broadened his perspective
and led him to eventually abandon concentration on the scientific aspects of education and to concentrate his efforts in the
sociological dimension of educational research.

During the 1920s, Counts's works reflected the impetus of
the scientific movement in education in that they were primarily statistical surveys. *The Senior High School Curricu-*
lum, The Social Composition of Boards of Education, and *The*
Selective Character of American Secondary Education all bore
the impress of the survey and sampling methods characteristic
of the scientific movement in education. However, even within

these early works, Counts began to reveal an increasing awareness of the importance of the implications of sociology for educational research. The most general characteristic of these early works as sociological studies was the indication of the class and economic consciousness which Counts felt permeated American education. These early works established a view of the selective character of education on a socio-economic class basis —a view that has persisted in contemporary educational literature. Nevertheless, the generalizations which Counts developed in these early works were all limited to specific educational situations and problems. By the end of the 1920s, Counts was delving more and more into the sociological aspects of education. *Secondary Education and Industrialism* contained a preview of Counts's future concentration on the impact of science and industrialism upon American society and education.

In addition to these more specific works, *The Principles of Education,* written in collaboration with J. Crosby Chapman, embodied a philosophical, psychological, and methodological overview of American education. This work of 1924 was permeated with the instrumentalist philosophy and habit psychology of John Dewey. During the 1920s, Counts seemed to share in the child-centered movement in progressive education. All observers, including Woelfel, Cremin, and Childs, place him within the instrumentalist philosophic orientation and within the ranks of the progressive educators.

By the depression period of the 1930s, Counts's educational writings took on a decidedly socio-historical cast. *The Social Foundations of Education* and *The Prospects of American Democracy* embraced the relativism of the "new history" and the instrumentalist educational philosophy. This combination of historical relativism and educational instrumentalism led to the development of the civilizational or cultural approach to educational theory. In the light of the economic pressures of the depression period, Counts's works took on the form of pleas for social, economic, and political reforms.

Early in the 1930s with his *Dare the School Build a New Social Order?*, Counts aggravated the split in the Progressive Education Association between the proponents of a child-centered school and the advocates of a socially oriented school. This split in the ranks of progressive educators that began in the 1930s continued until the dissolution of the Progressive Education Association in 1956. As one of the most articulate advocates of the socially oriented school, Counts received attention as the spokesmen for those who opposed concentration solely on the interests and needs of the child to the exclusion of social needs. He also criticized the advocates of the scientific movement in education and the educational methodologists. The works of the Commission on the Social Studies in the Schools of which Counts was research director also minimized the science of education, tests and measurements, and educational methodology. The Commission's reports were criticized by: one, those who defended the science of education; and two, those who attacked its radicalism.

Counts's works during the 1930s implied a form of social reconstructionism. While he proposed that the school build a new social order, Counts never indicated the precise formula which should be used to do so. Although a number of individuals in educational theory have advocated social reconstructionism since the 1930s, Counts has not made any further developments or contributions to this effort. Brameld implied that the pressures of World War II and the international tensions of the postwar period have occupied Counts's attention since the depression period of the 1930s. If Counts is to be associated with the later theoretical developments of the reconstructionists in education, it must be as a forerunner or pioneer rather than as a continuing contributor or persistent advocate.

Although most observers have associated Counts with the progressive movement in education, his major attention since World War II has been devoted to the study of Soviet Russian education. Although he has been a constant critic of the Communist educational program and practice, Counts has recognized the Soviet concentration on science and technology as a serious threat to the United States and Western Europe. Since World War II, Counts has written several books which were concerned with the problems of American education in the postwar world: *Education and the Promise of America, Education and American Civilization,* and *The Foundations of Human Freedom.* These later works have been concerned primarily with the problems of maintaining democratic liberties at a time when the nation is faced with a serious external threat. Although Counts paid some attention to economic problems in these works, he has been concerned chiefly with the preservation of the essential democratic political processes which have characterized the American experience. He has also been concerned with the problem of the realization of full equality of opportunity to all Americans and has been opposed to the violation of the civil liberties. In these later works, Counts has not seemed to fear economic concentration as a menace to democratic liberties to the degree that he did in the 1930s. Rather, he has focused attention on the power potentialities which lie within the military structure of the modern state. He has pointed out the impossibility of revolution against the powerful instruments of military technology. Although he has pointed out the dangers of military technology, he has not yet presented a proposed solution to the potential threat to democratic liberties. Nor has he taken up the problems of the intricacies of maintaining the democratic processes in a mass society.

In the 1950s, the Progressive Education Association, renamed the American Educational Fellowship, debated a statement of policy for the post–World War II period. Much of the discussion focused on two essential points: one, economic organization in an industrialized democracy; two, international organization in a world of atomic and nuclear weapons. A good deal of the discussion still centered about many of the points which Counts had raised in the 1930s.

Progressive Education stated that educational theorists were once again neglecting the economic problems of the postwar period as they had neglected these problems in the 1920s. The journal stated that during the 1930s some American educators became sufficiently concerned to voice their anger at economic tragedy through *Social Frontier* and the Commission of the American Historical Association on the Social Studies in the Schools. They had analyzed the failures of the system and demanded fundamental changes. *Progressive Education* observed, however, that, as the depression waned and the nation became preoccupied with the war effort, the voices of these educators had softened to a whisper: "It was almost as if those theorists were right who have said that the educator is always chiefly a reflector of the social order—rather than its critic, leader, and re-creator." [1]

Since World War II, Counts has changed his orientation from that of economic problems to the problems faced by the nation in the postwar world. The pleas for democratic collectivism have been stilled and replaced by pleas for civil liberties and the preservation of the democratic processes. However, one can still find the plea for a greater participation and sharing of all citizens in the material, cultural, and spiritual resources of the United States.

Counts realized that complete economic equality was a condition still far removed from the current American scene. His postwar works continued to point to the need for greater attempts to secure economic equality. However, the periods of social reform of the New and Fair Deals introduced legislation that provided economic safeguards and greater economic security for larger numbers of Americans. Although certainly not comprehensive nor complete in the sense of the pleas for a collectivistic economy, this legislation aided in removing much of the immediate menace presented by the dire insecurity of the depression period.

Many of the depression period pressures were directed to the obtaining of the essentials of economic life: food, clothing, shelter. Most of these pressures resulted from obvious and direct areas of economic insecurity. Although technological unemployment remained a problem in the postwar period, the nation has not experienced any situation comparable to the massive unemployment of the depression period. World War II, the Cold War, and increased consumer purchasing power reduced unemployment and produced economic prosperity.

This prosperity has caused the immediate economic concerns of many Americans to be satisfied. Despite the economic fulfillment enjoyed by many Americans, Counts has pointed to the economic deprivation of many racial and regional minorities and has argued for action to alleviate this deprivation. Essentially, the concerns of the nation in the domestic sphere have shifted from the immediate economic concerns to those of a qualitative democracy which permits greater sharing in the cultural, educational, and service aspects of civilization.

Paramount among these concerns of the postwar period was the guaranteeing of civil liberties and the removing of discrimination against certain citizens. In his postwar works, Counts has emphasized a qualitative sharing in American life by all rather than the earlier quantitative emphasis which demanded a more equalitarian distribution of the things necessary to satisfy basic life needs.

Counts used the operational premise that education is always conditioned by particular problems, places, times, and situations. The America of the 1950s and 1960s was not the same as the America of the 1930s. Many of the arguments of the depression period were no longer relevant to the age of international tension and insecurity produced by a bipolar power structure and the chronic threat of nuclear destruction. American education faced new pressures. These pressures were structured around the demand that the school aid in providing an education for national security in the wake of rising international tensions.

In finally assessing the role played by Counts in the 1930s, it must be said that this period represented a stage in the life of the man. To completely judge the theory of Counts solely by his works during the depression period in the light of the changed conditions of the 1960s would be to fail to place it in historical perspective. What can be said in fairness is that Counts, during the depression period, was truly a man of that crucial and crisis-ridden decade. He labored in the light of the problems of that period.

Although many of the considerations of Counts during the 1930s are no longer the pressing problems of the atomic age, certain features of the theory as developed during the depression remain significant to this age. First, the civilizational approach to education still remains a viable and significant approach to educational problems. However, this approach seems to have the disability of laboring in the persistence of cultural and educational lag. By the time Counts had formulated the specifics of his program, the social demands had already shifted to a new plane. Of course, Counts, like many others, preoccupied with pressing domestic economic problems, did not foresee the impact of the totalitarian movements on Western civilization in general, and on American democracy in particular. Still, the basic problem remains the ability to chart the course of social change and demands—a problem which is yet unsolved. Counts's theory was weak in that much of what seemed to be a social theory at the time was in reality a description of the problems of the period in their historical setting. The generalities and vagueness of many of the terms and concepts used by Counts posed a definite problem in their implementation as instruments of analysis. Despite these weaknesses, the civilizational approach to educational problems remains a significant contribution to educational theory. It created an awareness that education proceeded within the confines and limitations of a definite and particular social complex.

Secondly, the civilizational elements that Counts used as a frame of reference to his theory, democracy and technology, remain crucial components of American civilization. Counts performed a service by channelling the contributions of the "new history," and the contemporary sociological and educational research into language which fitted the needs of the depression period. To be sure, many of these investigations had importance for the 1930s and their usefulness is limited today. As the "new history" was based on a continuous reconstruction and reevaluation of events in the light of the present, so did educational theory become subject to constant reinterpretation and reevaluation in the light of changing conditions.

However, as instruments of social analysis and interpretation, Counts's discussion of the concepts of "democracy," "technology," "economic aristocracy," "collectivism," and even "imposition" failed to reach the point of precise definition. In retrospect, these terms seem to be descriptive or highly futuristic and lacking in precise definition. Even in the 1930s, these terms lacked the clarity necessary for their implementation as concepts for highly analytical social and educational analysis.

Although Counts's terminology and conceptual framework may be criticized as to its lack of precision by social and educational theorists, this terminology did provide a service to the classroom teachers and educational workers of the 1930s. The common-sense language used provided an easy vehicle of discussion of the current social and economic trends for use by the classroom teacher who was not an expert in social analysis. The attempt to translate current socio-economic trends into educational theory was neglected until the works of Counts and other like-minded educators during the depression period. Counts provided what can be regarded as a description and interpretation of socio-economic trends along the contours of the "new history" for the educational profession. However, when he attempted to predict or to offer generalizations, his proposals became clouded and vague. Although teachers appreciated the descriptions offered by Counts, many seemed to be confused about the right next steps to be taken both to advance democratic collectivism and to impose definite factual and evaluative criteria.

Although Counts's educational philosophy and program was structured around the concepts of democracy and technology and the advent of a collectivistic society, it lacked a precise formulation for attaining the desired ends. Although the descriptive materials embodied in the definitions of these terms were adequately explained and documented, the projections of these terminologies into the collectivistic future lacked the procedural methods necessary for their realization.

In his *Dare Progressive Education Be Progressive?*, Counts graphically called attention to the weaknesses of progressive education in completely relying on the child-centered school. His call for the specific imposition of democratic and cooperative values awoke many teachers to the reality that they were by their very teaching imposing certain social and political beliefs upon students. Counts urged that this imposition be deliberately done instead of approaching this problem haphazardly or unconsciously. He was part of the group of socially oriented educators such as John Childs who urged a deliberate imposition for democracy. However, once again the precise program of imposition failed to reach a high level of clarity and precision.

Somewhat more definite was Counts's approach to the problem of the social studies and the socially oriented curriculum. He favored the exposure of students to the various conflicts in the social, economic, and political spheres which characterized modern society. Students were to study and analyze the conflicts of the society since these constituted major social problems. The list of conflicts to be analyzed was influenced by the depression period milieu. Counts seemed to direct attention to an understanding, analysis, and appreciation of social problems. In this respect, he resembled his colleague Harold Rugg. Counts's emphasis on the study of social problems seemed to leave unanswered several questions: one, after the study of the social conflict areas what course of action was the student to follow. Were students to act upon social questions? Two, although conflict areas were to be analyzed and discussed, how were these conflict areas to be precisely resolved and adjudicated. Counts seemed to stress the traditional processes of political democracy for the resolution of economic and social conflicts. He failed to elaborate a precise methodology of adjudicating social conflicts. Despite these criticisms which were directed against Counts's program for social knowledge in the curriculum, the important contribution made by Counts in the social studies was the introduction of the analysis of these conflicts into the school. Controversial issues were not to be ignored nor avoided by the school. Rather, social conflicts were to be presented to the students for study and deliberation. It has been pointed out, however, that the areas of social problems rapidly shifted with changing social, political, and economic perspectives. Indeed, much of Counts's specific program of study was rendered inoperative by the change engendered by the shift from the depression era to war-time and then to the international tensions of the cold war period. In the light of these shifting social perspectives, the development of a precise method of analysis and criticism and adjudication may have been a greater contribution.

Before concluding this study of Counts's published works, it would be appropriate to turn to several criticisms which Albert Vogel made in the unpublished dissertation, "A Critical Analysis of the Major Writings of George S. Counts." Vogel criticized Counts in two areas: one, the failure to elaborate a world view or philosophy; and two, his eclecticism. It would seem that the first criticism does not apply to the frame of reference developed by Counts. Stressing social and educational relativism, Counts grounded his theory on the operational premises that education was always conditioned by a particular geographical, historical, and sociological environment. To attempt to formulate a world view or universalized philosophical orientation would have violated the very operational premises from which Counts proceeded. Vogel might have more justly criticized Counts's adherence to cultural relativism, but to criticize the theorist for being loyal to his operational premise seems unwarranted.

Secondly, Vogel criticized Counts for being an eclectic and drawing on materials from many secondary sources. It would seem that this criticism can be dealt with in two ways: one, that Counts used the research conclusions of contemporary historians, sociologists, economists, and educational theorists is undoubtedly true. Once again this synthesis which Counts attempted agreed with the interdisciplinary approach which Counts himself recommended for educational theory and practice.

On the other hand, Vogel may have implied that Counts failed to make an original contribution to the field of educational theory. As has been pointed out several times in this paper, Counts operated within the contours of a climate of opinion which was generated by the depression and its attendant pressures. Educational theorists such as John Dewey, Harold Rugg, John Childs, and William H. Kilpatrick also shared views similar to Counts during this time. Counts was part of a circle of educational and social theorists and did not operate in isolation from this milieu. He possessed the ability to use appealing and popular language and to illustrate pressing issues. This ability attracted attention to these issues and made him a center of controversy, criticism, and comment. He undoubtedly was a pioneer in developing the socially oriented approach to educational problems. He was also a leader in drawing generalizations and interpretations of a social nature during the 1930s. For this scholarship and effort, Counts won a prominent place in the annals of American social and educational history.

Conclusion

Although George S. Counts was a penetrating commentator on American society and education when he issued his famous challenge "Dare the School Build a New Social Order?," his contributions to American education were not confined to the depression era of the 1930s. In retrospect, Counts's critique of American education seems equally appropriate for the contemporary educator. Indeed, the rhetoric and programs of President Lyndon Johnson's "war on poverty" and quest for the "Great Society" were reminiscent of Counts's social and educational commentaries of the 1930s. Many of the problems which Counts cited in *The Prospects of American Democracy* in 1938 remain the unsolved problems which America still faces: racial discrimination, economic inequalities, academic freedom and dissent, war, poverty, pollution, and elitism. In many ways, Counts's pioneering work in the social foundations of education was prophetic of the continuing tasks which face American educators.

In 1969, on the occasion of his eightieth birthday, Counts wrote that we were living in "an age of revolution as wide as the planet." [2] In the light of rapid and revolutionary social change, the education which adequately served one generation might be inappropriate for another generation. Although Americans had crossed the watershed from an agricultural to an industrial society at the turn of the century, they had not yet created the education appropriate for life in an urbanized and industrialized society. Thus, Counts's query, "Dare the School Build a New Social Order?," still remained an open and unanswered question.

1. "A New Policy for New Times," *Progressive Education,* 25 (1948), 40–41.

2. George S. Counts, "Should the Teacher Always Be Neutral?" *Phi Delta Kappan* 51 (1969), 188.

Bibliography

Manuscripts and Letters

The manuscripts and letters cited in this section of the bibliography are in the personal library of Dr. George S. Counts, Southern Illinois University, Carbondale, Illinois.

Counts, George S. Letter to Dean William F. Russell. January 19, 1931.

————. "The Meaning of a Liberal Education in Industrial Society." Undated.

————. "A Proposal for Historical and Cultural Foundations at Columbia." Undated.

————. "A Proposal for the Establishment at Teachers College of an Institute for the Study of the Historical and Cultural Relations of American Education." Undated.

————. "Proposed Study of Education and Culture in an American Industrial Community." Undated.

————. "Some Thoughts on the Organization of an Institute of Social Research at Teachers College." Undated.

————. "Tentative Plan for the Organization of an Institute of Social Research at Teachers College." Undated.

Books

Beard, Charles A. *The Economic Basis of Politics*. New York: Alfred A. Knopf, 1934.

Beard, Charles A. *Economic Origins of Jeffersonian Democracy*. New York: Macmillan Co., 1927.

Beard, Charles and Mary. *America in Midpassage*. New York: Macmillan Co., 1939.

Becker, Carl L. *Progress and Power*. Stanford: Stanford University Press, 1935.

Bellamy, Edward. *Looking Backward.* New York: New American Library, 1960.

Berle, A. A. and Means, G. C. *The Modern Corporation and Private Property.* New York: Commerce Clearing House, 1932.

Brameld, Theodore. *Toward a Reconstructed Philosophy of Education.* New York: Dryden Press, 1956.

Burnham, James. *The Managerial Revolution.* New York: John Day Co., 1941.

Casson, Stanley. *Progress and Catastrophe.* New York: Harper & Bros. Publishers, 1937.

Chapman, J. Crosby and Counts, George S. *Principles of Education.* Chicago: Houghton Mifflin Co., 1924.

Chase, Stuart. *A New Deal.* New York: Macmillan Co., 1932.

Childs, John L. *American Pragmatism and Education.* New York: Henry Holt & Co., 1956.

Childs, John L. and Counts, George S. *America, Russia, and the Communist Party in the Postwar World.* New York: John Day Co., 1943.

Cole, G. D. H. *What Marx Really Meant.* New York: Alfred A. Knopf, 1937.

Committee of the Progressive Education Association on Social and Economic Problems. *A Call to the Teachers of the Nation.* New York: John Day Co., 1933.

Counts, George S. *The American Road to Culture: A Social Interpretation of Education in the United States.* New York: John Day Co., 1930.

————. *Dare the School Build a New Social Order?* New York: John Day Co., 1932.

————. *Educacao para uma sociedade de homens livres na era tecnologica.* Rio de Janeiro: Centro Brasileiro de Pesquisas educacionais, 1958.

————. *Education and American Civilization.* New York: Teachers College, Columbia University, Bureau of Publications, 1952.

————. *Education and the Foundations of Human Freedom.* Pittsburgh: University of Pittsburgh Press, 1962.

————. *Education and the Promise of America.* New York: Macmillan Co., 1946.

————. *The Prospects of American Democracy.* New York: John Day Co., 1938.

————. *School and Society in Chicago.* New York: Harcourt, Brace, & Co., 1928.

————. *The Schools Can Teach Democracy.* New York: John Day Co., 1939.

————. *Secondary Education and Industrialism.* Cambridge: Harvard University Press, 1929.

————. *The Selective Character of American Secondary Education.* Chicago: University of Chicago Press, 1922.

————. *The Senior High School Curriculum.* Chicago: University of Chicago Press, 1926.

————. *The Social Composition of Boards of Education.* Chicago: University of Chicago Press, 1927.

————. *The Social Foundations of Education.* New York: Charles Scribner's Sons, 1934.

————. *The Soviet Challenge to America.* New York: John Day Co., 1931.

Cremin, Lawrence A. *The Transformation of the School.* New York: Alfred A. Knopf, 1961.

Cremin, Lawrence A., Shannon, David A., and Townsend, Mary E. *A History of Teachers College Columbia University.* New York: Columbia University Press, 1954.

Curti, Merle. *The Social Ideas of American Educators.* Paterson, N.J.: Littlefield, Adams, and Co., 1959.

Dewey, John. *Art as Experience.* New York: G. P. Putnam's Sons, 1958.

————. *Democracy and Education.* New York: Macmillan Co., 1916.

Educational Policies Commission. *The Unique Function of Education in American Democracy.* Washington, D.C.: National Education Association, 1937.

Espy, Herbert C. *The Public Secondary School: A Critical Analysis of Secondary Education in the United States.* Chicago: Houghton Mifflin Co., 1939.

Hook, Sidney. *Towards the Understanding of Karl Marx.* London: Victor Gallancz, 1933.

Hoover, Herbert. *Addresses Upon the American Road, 1933–1938.* New York: Charles Scribner's Sons, 1938.

———. *The Memoirs of Herbert Hoover: The Great Depression, 1929–1941.* New York: Macmillan Co., 1952.

Hutchins, Robert M. *The Higher Learning in America.* New Haven: Yale University Press, 1936.

Iversen, Robert. *The Communists and the Schools.* New York: Harcourt, Brace, & Company, 1959.

Kandel, Isaac. *Conflicting Theories of Education.* New York: Macmillan Co., 1938.

Knight, Edgar W. *Education in the United States.* New York: Ginn and Co., 1934.

Mason, Robert E. *Educational Ideas in American Society.* Boston: Allyn and Bacon Co., 1960.

Meyer, Adolph E. *The Development of Education in the Twentieth Century.* Englewood Cliffs, N.J.: Prentice-Hall, 1949.

My Friends: Twenty-eight History Making Speeches by Franklin Delano Roosevelt. Edited by Edward H. Kavinoky and Julian Park. Buffalo, N.Y.: Foster and Stewart Publishing Co., 1945.

Nothing to Fear: The Selected Addresses of Franklin Delano Roosevelt, 1932–1945. Edited by B. D. Zevin. Cambridge, Mass.: Riverside Press, 1946.

Padover, Saul K. *The Genius of America.* New York: McGraw-Hill Book Co., 1960.

Plamenatz, John. *German Marxism and Russian Communism.* New York: Longmans, Green, & Co., 1954.

President's Research Committee on Social Trends. *Recent Social Trends in the United States.* New York: McGraw-Hill Co., 1933.

Rauch, Basil. *The History of the New Deal, 1933–1938.* New York: Creative Age Press, 1944.

Rugg, Harold. *The Great Technology.* New York: John Day Co., 1933.

Strout, Cushing. *The Pragmatic Revolt in American History: Carl Becker and Charles Beard.* New Haven: Yale University Press, 1958.

Toward Civilization. Edited by Charles A. Beard. New York: Longmans, Green, & Co., 1930.

Yesipov, B. P. and Goncharov, N. K. *I Want to be Like Stalin.* Translated with an introduction by George S. Counts and Nucia P. Lodge. New York: John Day Press, 1947.

Woelfel, Norman. *Molders of the American Mind.* New York: Columbia University Press, 1933.

Newspapers

Bridgeport (Conn.) *Telegram,* September 18, 1934.

Indianapolis News, September 22, 1934.

New York Times, September 18, 1934.

Articles

"The Association Faces its Opportunities," *Progressive Education,* 9 (1932), 229–331.

Bode, Boyd H. "Dr. Bode Replies," *The Social Frontier,* 2 (1935), 42–43.

Carlson, Avis D. "Deflating the Schools," *Harper's Monthly Magazine*, 167 (1933), 705–13.

Charters, W. W., Jr. "Social Class Analysis and the Control of Public Education," *The Sociology of Education*. Edited by Robert R. Bell. Homewood, Ill.: Dorsey Press, 1962, pp. 174–90.

Clapp, Elsie Ripley. "Learning and Indoctrinating," *Progressive Education*, 9 (1932), 269–72.

"Collectivism and Collectivism," *The Social Frontier*, 1 (1934), 3–4.

Counts, George S. "Business and Education," *Teachers College Record*, 39 (1938), 553–60.

————. "Dare Progressive Education Be Progressive?" *Progressive Education*, 9 (1932), 257–63.

————. "Education and the Five Year Plan of Soviet Russia," *National Education Association Proceedings*, 68 (1930), 213–18.

————. "Education—For What?: The Ten Fallacies of the Educators," *New Republic*, 71 (1932), 12–16.

————. "A Liberal Looks At Life," *Frontiers of Democracy*, 7 (1941), 231–32.

————. "The Place of the School in the Social Order," *National Education Association Proceedings*, 64 (1926), 308–15.

————. "Presentday Reasons for Requiring a Longer Period of Pre-Service Preparation for Teachers," *National Education Association Proceedings*, 73 (1935), 694–701.

————. "Rally Around AFT Program—Acceptance Speech," *American Teacher*, 24 (1939), 1–2.

————. "Secondary Education and the Social Problem," *School Executives Magazine*, 51 (August, 1932), 499–501, 519–20.

————. "Should the Teacher Always Be Neutral?," *Phi Delta Kappan*, 51 (1969), 186–89.

————. "Theses on Freedom, Culture, Social Planning and Leadership," *National Education Association Proceedings*, 70 (1932), 249–52.

————. "To Vitalize American Tradition," *Progressive Education,* 15 (1938), 245.

————. "What is a School of Education?" *Teachers College Record,* 30 (1929), 647–55.

————. "Who Shall Make the Curriculum?" *School Review,* 35 (1927), 332–39.

Cummings, Milton C. "How Can the Schools Build a New Social Order," *School and Society,* 36 (1932), 756–58.

De Lima, Agnes. "Education—For What: Reply to George S. Counts," *New Republic,* 71 (1932), 317.

Dewey, John. "Can Education Share in Social Reconstruction?" *Social Frontier,* 1 (1934), 12.

"Economics and the Good Life," *Social Frontier,* 2 (1935), 72–73.

"Educating For Tomorrow," *Social Frontier,* 1 (1934), 5–7.

"Freedom in a Collectivistic Society," *Social Frontier,* 1 (1935), 9–10.

Geer, Ellen W. "The Courage to Keep an Open Mind," *Progressive Education,* 9 (1932), 265–67.

Holmes, Henry. "The Teacher in Politics," *Progressive Education,* 9 (1932), 414–18.

"Introductory Remarks on Indoctrination," *Social Frontier,* 1 (1935), 8–9.

"Notes on the Convention," *Progressive Education,* 9 (1932), 288–91.

"A New Policy for New Times," *Progressive Education,* 25 (1948), 40–41.

"Orientation," *The Social Frontier,* 1 (1934), 3–5.

"The Position of the Social Frontier," *Social Frontier,* 1 (1935), 30–33.

Read, Conyers, "The Social Responsibilities of the Historian," *American Historical Review,* 55 (1950), 275–85.

Seeds, Nellie M. "Educating for Social Change," *Progressive Education,* 9 (1932), 267–69.

Sorenson, Lloyd R. "Charles A. Beard and German Historical Thought," *Mississippi Valley Historical Review*, 42 (1953), 275–85.

"Teachers and the Class Struggle," *Social Frontier*, 2 (1935), 39–40.

"Unmentionable Counts," *Time*, 28 (1936), 66–68.

Varney, Harold L. "Class War on the Campus," *American Mercury*, 40 (1937), 462–72.

Unpublished Materials

Durnin, Sister Mary C. "The Educational Philosophy of George S. Counts." Unpublished master's dissertation, Catholic University of America, Washington, D.C., 1940.

Vogel, Albert W. "A Critical Study of the Major Writings of George S. Counts." Unpublished Ed.D. dissertation, American University, Washington, D.C., 1960.

Other Sources

Personal interview with George S. Counts. December, 1963.

Index